From Dominoes to Dynamos

From Dominoes to Dynamos

The Transformation of Southeast Asia

John Bresnan

COUNCIL ON FOREIGN RELATIONS PRESS

NEW YORK

COUNCIL ON FOREIGN RELATIONS BOOKS

If you would like more information on Council publications, please write the Council on Foreign Relations, 58 East 68th Street, New York, NY 10021, or call the Publications Office at (212) 734-0400.

Library of Congress Cataloging-in-Publication Data

Bresnan, John, 1927–
    From dominoes to dynamos: the transformation of Southeast Asia/
John Bresnan.
        p.   cm.
Includes bibliographical references and index.
ISBN 0-87609-166-4: $17.95
    1. Asia, Southeastern—Economic conditions. 2. Asia,
Southeastern—Social conditions. 3. United States—Relations—Asia,
Southeastern. 4. Asia, Southeastern—Relations—United States.
I. Title.
HC441.B74   1994
330.959'053—dc20   94-11497
                                                              CIP

94   95   96   97   98   EB   10   9   8   7   6   5   4   3   2   1

This book is dedicated to
Evelyn Colbert and James W. Morley—
scholars, mentors, friends

Contents

Acknowledgments

Although I first went to Southeast Asia to live and work more than thirty years ago and have followed the affairs of the region more or less continuously ever since as a foundation executive and university scholar, I am nonetheless very much indebted to many others in writing this book about the region and America's relations with it.

At the Council on Foreign Relations, Peter Tarnoff, then president, took an early interest in the need for a fresh American view of Southeast Asia; Nicholas X. Rizopoulos, vice president of the Council's Studies Department, commissioned the study in 1991; Alan D. Romberg, then senior fellow, directed the study group on Southeast Asia that met in 1992, and was my single most valuable supporter and critic throughout the writing of the book; Dianne Schwartz served as staff to the project; Jonathan Stromseth was the study group rapporteur; Judith Train edited the book. I thank them for enlisting me in the project and for helping me bring it to a conclusion in this volume.

The study group on Southeast Asia, which met in 1992, was an invaluable resource to me, as I am sure it was to its other members. I wish to express my particular thanks to Robert A. Scalapino, who served as chairman of the study group at considerable inconvenience to himself, for his unflagging interest and wise counsel. I thank the following members who took part in meetings or sent written comments on drafts I prepared for discussion: Morton I. Abramowitz, Stephen W. Bosworth, Marshall M. Bouton, Lawrence Brainard, Frederick Z. Brown, William P. Bundy, Robert

Case, Nayan Chanda, Evelyn Colbert, Kenneth W. Dam, David B. H. Denoon, Robert P. DeVecchi, William Drayton, Jr., S. R. Foley, Jr., Theodore Friend, Jeffrey E. Garten, William H. Gleysteen, Jr., Sidney R. Jones, Stanley Karnow, Robert H. Legvold, Robert Manning, Jonathan Moore, James W. Morley, Marvin C. Ott, Hugh T. Patrick, Russell A. Phillips, Jr., James Przystup, Kenneth Quinn, Stanley O. Roth, Richard W. Sonnenfeldt, Herman Starobin, and Charles Wolf, Jr. I also thank the following people who participated as guests of the study group, some travelling a considerable distance to do so: Narongchai Akrasanee, Muthiah Alagappa, Allen Choate, Donald Emmerson, Eugene Matthews, Charles Morrison, Pang Eng Fong, Sukhumbhand Paribatra, Hadi Soesastro, Richard H. Solomon, Strobe Talbott, and Casimir Yost. One can only hope this book reflects in some measure the value of the contributions these many individuals made to their mutual understanding and to my own.

The Council also convened a meeting in April 1993, to review the first draft of the book manuscript. I thank the members of this review group for their helpful service to me: Robert Scalapino, who chaired the group; Alan Romberg, who directed the review; and those who participated either in person or in writing: C. Michael Aho, Frederick Z. Brown, Evelyn Colbert, David B. H. Denoon, William H. Gleysteen, Jr., Erland Heginbotham, Lawrence B. Krause, James Morley, Marvin C. Ott, Dwight Perkins, James Przystup, Stanley O. Roth, and Sheldon Simon. Any remaining errors of fact, interpretation, or judgment that remain are, of course, my own.

The project as a whole was made possible by the generous support of the Rockefeller Brothers Fund. The Pacific Basin Studies Program at Columbia University made possible the commitment of my time to the study, as well as my travel in the region for interviews.

Many diplomats, military officers, trade officials, business people, and others spoke to me in off-the-record meetings in Bangkok, Jakarta, Kuala Lumpur, Manila, and Singapore, as well as in Washington and New York. I trust they will find their views reflected faithfully here.

The title of this book is taken from the remarks of President Bill Clinton to the host committee for the Asia Pacific Economic Cooperation meeting in Seattle on November 19, 1993.

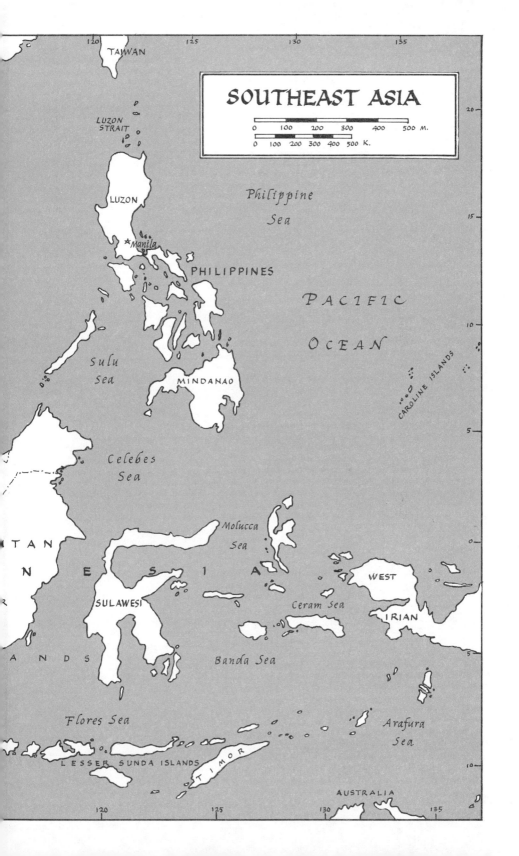

Chapter 1

Introduction

As the United States reassesses its moral and material interests in the wake of the Cold War, Southeast Asia demands Washington's early and earnest attention. It is a major world region, the demographic equal of Latin America or Africa, and Americans have played a significant role there for most of the past century. All through the Cold War, American governments viewed Southeast Asia as strategic to U.S. security, and many states of the region stood firmly at the side of the United States. The United States helped many of these same states to achieve record economic growth and become major trading partners. Now, the lone superpower, the United States needs to decide afresh the meaning of the region to itself. It must do so promptly, because Southeast Asians are rapidly reassessing their interests in the United States.

The past American role in Southeast Asia has been defined very largely in military and strategic terms. The United States was a colonial power in the Philippines from the turn of the century, defeated the Japanese occupiers of the region from Burma to Indonesia in the early 1940s, and participated in the most costly fighting of the Cold War in Indochina in the late 1960s and early 1970s. Americans paid little notice in recent years as the United States left its last base in the Philippines and opened talks with Vietnam, but in Southeast Asia it was abundantly clear that an era had ended. The

1

region is in search of a new security system, and leaders there are hoping the United States will play a role in the process. U.S. policymakers need to redefine the security role they seek. Southeast Asia is one region in which American policy will be tested by friends and allies who have known the United States through bad times as well as good, and are eager for it to stay.

The Clinton administration came to office arguing that creating more jobs in the American economy is of equal importance to helping the international community oppose aggression. The economic choice is clear. If the United States is going to spur its economic growth, it must do so by increasing government spending or by expanding the nation's exports. And Southeast Asia is a prime target for expansion of U.S. exports; it already is a market for more U.S. exports than South America, the Middle East, or the former Soviet Union and eastern Europe. One reason is that the economies of Southeast Asia have been among the most rapidly growing in the world in recent decades, and can afford to buy what the United States has to sell. U.S. exports to Southeast Asia must increase if the balance in U.S. trade across the Pacific as a whole is to improve. Washington needs to pursue a strategy to do that.

Meanwhile human rights have rapidly become a topic of contention in U.S. dealings with Southeast Asia. It was predictable that, with the Cold War over, the region's authoritarian political regimes would have less of a hold on American support. But the degree of disagreement owes much also to differences in public attitudes toward government: Americans tend to expect little from theirs, and Southeast Asians have much to be thankful for from theirs. The result has been that friendly governments of Southeast Asia have joined with China and Vietnam to challenge American views on human rights. Abuses of human rights are occurring in the region, and the United States must work to prevent them. But the United States cannot be effective so long as almost all the states of the region are aligned against it. The United States needs a human rights policy in Southeast Asia that meets expectations both at home and among friendly critics in the region.

Another issue Washington must address is that whereas the United States has customarily dealt with the states of Southeast Asia individually, now these nations themselves are moving American policymakers to develop a view of the region as a whole. The Association of Southeast Asian Nations (ASEAN)—made up of the noncommunist states of Brunei, Indonesia, Malaysia, the Philippines, Singapore, and Thailand—has a history of twenty-five years of peaceful relations among its members. The ASEAN states led the international diplomatic effort to end the Vietnamese occupation of Cambodia. They have been crucial to the founding of the Asia Pacific Economic Cooperation forum, the first organization of governments that spans the Pacific from east to west and north to south. They are the sponsors of the new ASEAN Regional Forum, the first instance of official multilateral talks on the security of the Pacific. Given their key role in the movement toward a Pacific community, the United States must learn quickly how to respond to the ASEAN nations collectively, as well as individually.

As the only superpower in the new world order, the United States is unparalleled in its power. Yet the end of the Cold War, while it has enhanced American influence in eastern Europe and the former Soviet Union, has reduced American influence in other regions. In the Asia-Pacific region, the United States will strive to sustain a partnership with Japan and China, because the stakes are so high it cannot afford to do otherwise. One must be less confident about relations with Southeast Asia. Already Southeast Asians see the United States as a declining factor in their affairs, either because the latter is consciously withdrawing or because others are a rising and more congenial economic and political presence. The major question hanging over Southeast Asia's future is what role the United States will fashion for itself in the region's affairs.

The United States has extensive economic, political, and strategic interests in the region. Now is the time for it to articulate a policy to sustain them. This study aims to evaluate these interests, analyze the challenges confronting them, and lay out a framework for policies designed to protect and advance them. Southeast Asia is undergoing economic and social change at a pace unrivaled in the world. Positioning itself to deal with that change is a task that the United States should begin now.

Chapter 2

Reckoning the American Interest

The United States has substantial interests in Southeast Asia. They are centered in the five major noncommunist states of the region—Indonesia, Malaysia, the Philippines, Singapore, and Thailand—which, along with Brunei, make up ASEAN. These states have a combined population of more than 300 million people, or almost three-fourths of the population of Southeast Asia. They account for 90 percent of the region's economic product. And they share extensive strategic, political, economic, and social interests with the United States.

U.S. economic interests are now among Washington's most important foreign policy concerns. In the case of Southeast Asia, these economic interests are substantial; they are as large as or larger than U.S. economic interests in many other regions of the world. U.S. exports to the ASEAN countries exceed those to any other region in the world except northeast Asia and western Europe. And the ASEAN market for goods and services that the United States wants to sell is growing rapidly. If the American economy is to be improved without increasing budget spending, exports will have to expand. Since exports do best where markets are expanding, that means increasing exports to Southeast Asia. Failure to make this a high priority could prove costly to the national economy.

At issue is whether the United States will continue to be a principal partner of the Southeast Asian economies—whether it will be squeezed out by Japan, Taiwan, South Korea, and China, or will organize itself to compete more effectively. There is more opinion on this topic than hard data. Assessing the situation accurately with regard to the scale of U.S., Japanese, and other investment is problematic. Establishing the extent to which governments may use political and economic subsidies to explain export sales is difficult. Nevertheless, many U.S. business leaders view their competition in Southeast Asia with the East Asians—and particularly with the Japanese—as a major test of the country's global capability.

Meanwhile, a significant side benefit to the United States from its relationship with the market economies of Southeast Asia has been their demonstration effect. The ASEAN states have been committed to mixed economies with large and growing private sectors, and have been increasingly open to economic competition from outside. These policy regimes, and their association with the economies of the United States and Japan, have had much to do with Southeast Asia's rapid economic growth. This dramatic performance, in countries that account for more than 300 million people, has had a powerful impact on others. The leaders of Vietnam have actively sought to learn from experienced policymakers in the ASEAN governments in charting their own economic reforms. But more broadly, as well, the United States has found some of its most impressive examples of the value of market-oriented economic policies among the ASEAN countries.

The social implications of the economic growth in Southeast Asia for U.S.–Southeast Asian relations are equally striking. Employment is shifting out of agriculture and into industry, populations are becoming more urban, average incomes are now largely in the middle-income range, savings and investment rates are running from 20 percent to 30 percent per annum, and the middle class in every capital city is demanding a larger role in government. The region's political record is not all positive, but this might bear little relevance for the future. Recent economic and social changes have produced conditions in several Southeast Asian states that already are similar to those of Korea and Taiwan a decade or so ago, with growing middle classes pressing for more open politics.

If the U.S. political interest is defined in terms of the openness of government and its responsiveness to society's demands, then the prognosis in much of Southeast Asia is positive. Discussion of public policy in the ASEAN states is much more open today than it was a decade ago, and income distribution is more equitable than in, say, Central or South America. At the same time, the transition from the authoritarian regimes of the past will not be smooth, as coups and attempted coups in the Philippines and Thailand have shown. U.S. influence can make a difference, however, as responses to U.S. protests over army shootings of political demonstrators in Bangkok and East Timor have made clear. In short, the United States can look on Southeast Asia as a major world region in which civil rights and social equity have relatively good prospects by world standards.

The economic growth of the past generation has had added repercussions in social relations with the United States. American business firms are represented on the ground in Southeast Asia in very large numbers. The U.S. chambers of commerce in most capitals of the region have memberships that run between 400 and 500. At the same time, the elites of these cities, increasingly wealthy, are educating their children in American colleges and universities in record numbers. These students numbered almost 50,000 in one recent year—more than the number from western Europe, Latin America, or any other region of the world except northeast Asia. Thus the most important social interactions occurring today between the United States and Southeast Asia are of a new kind, involving professional people, acting privately, with minimal involvement of government on either side.

Southeast Asia's economic success also has meant that these states can be valuable allies of the United States on the world stage: they tend to see eye to eye with the United States on a wide range of international issues. The United Nations–sponsored settlement in Cambodia, in which Indonesia and Thailand were intimately involved, and the UN-sanctioned response to the Iraqi invasion of Kuwait, which Malaysia supported in the Security Council, are only two major recent examples. Although not fully appreciated by the United States, Indonesia's leadership of the nonaligned movement also has had a strong moderating effect on a grouping that at one time was stridently anti-American. Furthermore, shared perspectives should provide a basis for more common action on a wide range of global issues in which the United States has a strong and direct interest, from environmental protection to drug control.

This shared perspective extends to regional security. The system of security built around the U.S. navy and its base at Subic Bay is no more. U.S. statements of its intention to remain a naval power in the region ring hollow in the light of the continuing budget problems in Washington. Yet easy access to and through Southeast Asia is important to the United States; air transit played a more significant role in the Gulf War than is generally recognized, and air and naval transit would have become much more significant if the war had dragged on. For the short term, the United States and Singapore have worked out a naval access agreement. Air agreements with Thailand and Singapore might prove even more significant for the future, with the likely emphasis in U.S. strategy on rapid deployment of combat units. But naval agreements with Indonesia and Malaysia are politically important, as well. The ASEAN states have been saying by these actions that they do not want the United States to leave the region precipitously, that they want it to be part of the transition to some new regional order. Having played a role in Southeast Asian affairs since Commodore George Dewey's fleet sank the Spanish fleet in Manila Bay in 1898, the United States has an interest in participating in this process.

The possibility of major conflict in the region seems remote. The principal source of potential instability would be a breakdown in security relations between the United States and Japan. The concern is that Japan might become unable to count on the United States to guarantee its security for any of a number of reasons, possibly associated with the imbalance in trade relations. If forced to "go it alone," Japan might feel obliged to arm itself with nuclear weapons and with missiles to deliver them. It also might feel obliged to extend its ability to project its naval power so as to protect its oil supply line from the Middle East. Avoiding such a scenario is a major American, as well as Southeast Asian, strategic interest.

China also is a potential source of strategic concern. The leadership succession in Beijing could again create major shifts in Chinese policy. The new generation of younger leaders lacks the legitimacy, broad ties, and general skills of the octogenarians they are replacing. And economic reform is creating widening gaps in income after decades of official commitment to socialist norms. This is not a formula for stability. Moreover, China's threat to tear up its agreement with the United Kingdom if it did not get its way on interim political reforms in Hong Kong was a reminder of China's ability to destabilize the region, as was the 1992 passage of legislation claiming much of the South China Sea as Chinese. The United States has a strategic interest in a strong Southeast Asia that can provide some balance to Chinese power.

The American strategic interest in Southeast Asia includes an interest in the region's capacity for multilateral action. The states of Southeast Asia have been highly effective in working together as members of ASEAN. They were crucial to the creation of the organization Asia Pacific Economic Cooperation, the first intergovernmental association linking the United States with East Asia, Southeast Asia, and Oceania. And they have taken the initiative in sponsoring talks with the United States and Japan, and prospectively with China and Russia, as well, regarding regional security issues. The United States can take some credit for the resilience of the ASEAN states, and it surely has an interest in their continued self-confidence.

U.S. interest in a strong and self-confident Southeast Asia also translates into U.S. interest in the normalization of relations with Vietnam. This is a nation of the region with which the United States has been deeply and tragically involved in the past, and with which the United States has deep grievances stemming from that past. These grievances might not find adequate satisfaction at any time soon. Be that as it may, bringing official relations to normalcy would benefit the region and the United States.

This reckoning of American interests is strikingly different from any that might have been written in earlier decades. The new agenda does not include any concern about near-term security threats to the United States or any of its friends and allies in Southeast Asia from any quarter. It is a more peaceable agenda than Americans have known in this region of the world since the years before World War II. It contains less of a focus on unilateral American action, especially since Bill Clinton's election to the presidency, and more on joint action with other nations. It gives less attention to what government must do, and more to what government and business can do, acting together. This is an agenda that depends very much on how American society performs at home; on stemming the loss of national savings through the federal budget; on redirecting Americans' thinking about trade toward exporting more, rather than importing less; on reestablishing social solidarity at home. It is not an agenda peculiar to American interests in Southeast Asia. But considering how this new American agenda is to be pursued in Southeast Asia will reveal a lot about how ready Americans are to change course, reorder priorities, and meet the challenges of the new era.

Chapter 3

Comprehending Southeast Asia

Pursuing American interests in Southeast Asia requires clarity of mind not only about the United States itself. At key points in its century-long history in Southeast Asia, the United States seriously misjudged the situations in the Philippines and in Vietnam. If U.S. policy in the future is not to rest on so tenuous a basis of comprehension as in the past, Americans need to have a different view of the region than they have had.

Southeast Asia is clearly demarcated physically, set off from China to the north and India to the west by the almost impenetrable eastern Himalayas, and bounded on the south and east by the massive volcanic arcs of the great Indonesian and Philippine archipelagoes. Culturally the region is divided broadly between the speakers of Burmese, Thai, and Vietnamese, who have been moving southward until historically recent times, and who now occupy the bulk of mainland Southeast Asia, and the speakers of Austronesian languages, who are the longer established peoples of the two great island groups.

The spread of Hinduism and Buddhism during the first millennium, and the spread of Islam from the late thirteenth century, heavily influenced much of Southeast Asia. This history left predominantly Buddhist populations in what is now Burma, Thailand, Cambodia, Laos, and Vietnam, and predominantly Muslim populations in Indonesia, Malaysia, and the southern Philippines. The colonial period saw the further differentiation of the region into colonies held at one time or another by Portugal, Spain, the Netherlands, Britain, France, and the United States; only Thailand remained independent. The same period saw the Christianization of the bulk of the Philippines and of minorities elsewhere. The resulting array of populations, divided by ethnicity, language, religion, and political history, is vastly more complex than that in Latin America and is perhaps even more complex than that in Africa.

The colonial period fragmented even the study of the region, as the British studied Burma; the French, Indochina; the Dutch, the East Indies; and so on, each group writing in its own language. The term "Southeast Asia" came into general use only during the Second World War, when the region was briefly united under Japanese occupation. In addition, when colonialists wrote about the region, they wrote principally about its responses to themselves. When an international team of scholars published a history of the region as recently as 1971, they titled it *In Search of Southeast Asia.*[1] Some cultural unity is only now beginning to enter the scene as a result of the spread of the use of English, which is the language of international discourse of the region, and the spread of cosmopolitan lifestyles among the national elites.

Americans came late to Southeast Asia. U.S. trade with China prospered after Chinese ports were opened in the 1840s. An American admiral, Matthew Perry, forced the opening of trade with Japan in 1854. But it was not until 1898, after the United States had gone to war with Spain in support of a rebellion in Cuba, that Americans entered Southeast Asia in any significant way. In May of that year, Commodore George Dewey sailed into Manila Bay and quickly defeated the Spanish fleet there. The victory made the United States a naval presence, albeit a modest one, in the western Pacific.

Americans had only limited knowledge of the Philippines at the start. President William McKinley proclaimed that he had no choice but "to educate the Filipinos, and uplift and civilize and Christianize them,"[2] not realizing that a great many of them were Christians already. A rebellion for national independence was under way in the Philippines, and Dewey's naval victory was followed by an ugly war that proved costly in lives and money. The fighting placed the Americans in need of Filipino allies, and thus began a marriage of convenience between American interests and the Filipino landed elite that lasted until the very recent past.[3]

The war with Japan from 1941 to 1945 did not lead to a wider U.S. involvement with Southeast Asia, although the Japanese occupied the entire region. The United States opted to avoid the populous areas of the region, with the exception of the Philippines, choosing instead to fight its way up the island chain of the western Pacific to the home islands of Japan. At the war's end, the United States also was reluctant to involve itself in the independence struggles that broke out in Indonesia and Indochina. U.S. policy in the immediate postwar period favored Europe as the first priority of the United States and, in Asia, favored Japan, Korea, and China. The United States nevertheless did in time come to play a significant role in the recognition of Indonesia's independence, in part because there was an established noncommunist leadership to support. In the case of Vietnam, on the other hand, although believing that French policy was playing into the hands of Vietnamese communists, the United States chose to support France in the interest of U.S. postwar aims in Europe.[4]

After the fall of the French garrison at Dien Bien Phu in 1954, an international conference in Geneva reached a settlement partitioning Vietnam into a communist north and noncommunist south. The United States had little confidence in the settlement; the "domino theory" described the common concern of American officials at the time that, in the absence of united action to contain them, the communists would eventually dominate Indochina, Thailand, and Burma. Before 1955 was out, on American initiative, the governments of Australia, France, New Zealand, Pakistan, the Philippines, Thailand, the United Kingdom, and the United States formed the Southeast Asia Treaty Organization (SEATO). The inclusion of Thailand represented the first American security commitment to the Southeast Asian mainland.[5]

The American military buildup in Vietnam a decade later reflected continuing official concern that the stakes involved were very high, including the independence of Thailand and confidence in American commitments elsewhere. But the 1965 decision to commit major American ground forces led to the loss of 58,000

American lives, divided American society more deeply than any event since the U.S. Civil War, and destroyed the presidency of Lyndon Johnson. The war was more costly still to Vietnam. That country experienced the loss of one million lives, the destruction of much of its physical infrastructure, the imposition of a harsh regime on the people of the south, and the flight of more than 500,000 people.[6]

Yet the outcome was full of ironies. The Vietnamese did attempt to establish their dominance over the rest of Indochina, invading Cambodia in 1978, and causing Thailand to feel seriously threatened. Help came from Thailand's noncommunist neighbors in the region—Indonesia, Malaysia, the Philippines, and Singapore—now organized in ASEAN. These nations together mobilized much international opinion against Vietnam. In time the Soviet Union joined the international consensus, leading to the withdrawal of Vietnamese troops in 1989. By this time it also was clear that the command economy imposed on Vietnam was not working, and economic reforms were begun that in effect discarded the Soviet model. The final irony was that the United States had little to do with these developments. Consumed for years by their bitter debate over Vietnam, Americans in defeat had turned their attention away from Southeast Asia. Even American scholarly work on Southeast Asia, never strong, suffered from the "Vietnam syndrome."

Since the fall of Saigon in 1975, Washington's attention has been drawn back to the region only briefly, at moments of high drama. The principal occasion was in 1986, when Corazon Aquino faced Ferdinand Marcos in an election for the presidency of the Philippines; fraud was widespread, leaders of the armed forces declared for Mrs. Aquino, the middle class of Manila took to the streets in a display of "people power," and Marcos was obliged to flee to political refuge in the United States. The last-minute switch of American support to Mrs. Aquino was not enough to erase the feelings in Manila's political circles over the long-term American support of Marcos; in 1992 the Philippine Senate voted down a resolution to continue American access to its Subic Bay naval base, effectively ending the "special relationship" between the two countries.

In these circumstances Southeast Asia remains little studied as a region. It is still a surprise for some American policy analysts to discover that the population of Southeast Asia is slightly larger than that of Latin America and the Caribbean, and is only somewhat smaller than the population of Sub-Saharan Africa (see Table 1). It also is still a surprise for some Americans to discover that the market economies of Southeast Asia have been among the most rapidly growing in the world since the mid-1960s. As Table 1 shows, the gross domestic product (GDP) of Southeast Asia grew more than fourteen times between 1965 and 1990, while that of Latin America grew less than ten times, and that of much of Asia and Africa only five or six times. The result has been that the GDP of Southeast Asia (even excluding Vietnam, for which data are lacking) is rapidly approaching the GDP of China, is almost twice that of Africa, and in per capita terms separates Southeast Asia significantly from much of the rest of Asia. Perhaps the relative demographic and economic scale of Southeast Asia has been obscured in part by the bureaucratic practice, in the U.S. government and many international organizations, of melding Southeast Asia in with the rest of East Asia, which includes the demographic and economic behemoths of China and Japan. Thus, the Southeast Asia that we have not known is the Southeast Asia that has not entered into our calculations.

The capacity for misjudgment will always be there, built in to the structure of power relationships. But the state of our knowledge of Southeast Asia is remediable, and improvement is already under way in some areas. Within the U.S. government, American interests are particularly well served by the new generation of Vietnam War veterans in the Congress. The U.S. mass media, finding the region growing as a market, have improved their reporting somewhat in the past decade. U.S. manufacturing and service firms are increasingly well served by public and private market reporting and analysis. U.S. financial institutions are highly active in tracking investment opportunities, especially on behalf of the new and numerous country and regional funds. Nongovernmental organizations are active in reporting on behalf of numerous specialized interests, such as human rights and environmental protection. There are grounds to be hopeful about the future.

TABLE 1—POPULATION AND GROSS DOMESTIC PRODUCT (GDP): REGIONAL COMPARISONS

Region	Population (millions), mid-1990	GDP (millions of dollars), 1965	GDP (millions of dollars), 1990	GDP increase (in multiples), 1965–1990	GNP (dollars per capita), 1990
Southeast Asia	436.9	21,350*	309,190*	14.4*	690*
China	1,133.7	67,200	364,900	5.4	370
India	849.5	50,530	254,540	5.0	350
Sub-Saharan Africa	495.2	27,350	162,740	6.0	340
Latin America and Caribbean	433.1	102,480	1,015,160	9.9	2,180

Source: World Bank, *World Development Report 1992* (New York: Oxford University Press, 1992), Tables 1 and 3.

*Excludes Burma, Cambodia, Laos, and Vietnam, for which data are unavailable.

At the same time, serious constraints remain. Americans are as a nation more familiar with the Philippines and Vietnam than with the Southeast Asian countries where U.S. economic interests are highest—Indonesia, Thailand, Malaysia, and Singapore. Within the U.S. government, these states face a continual lack of attention because they are bureaucratically competitive with China and Japan, and because the U.S. diplomatic corps is weak in business and economic know-how. The first generation of American academic specialists on Southeast Asia, relatively small in number, who appeared in U.S. universities in the 1950s, are now retiring and are not being replaced. So there is action that is needed, and needed promptly, if the United States is to change course as a nation, leave the priorities of the Cold War behind, and pursue a new national agenda.

The United States needs as a nation to alter the balance of its intellectual and bureaucratic resources so as to give more adequate attention to Southeast Asia as a whole, especially in agencies concerned with foreign economic relations. As an indication of the direction in which the United States needs to be thinking if it is to remain competitive, the Departments of State and Commerce ought seriously to consider the resources the government of Japan has devoted to Southeast Asia. The United States also should move promptly to alter the balance within the resources it devotes to Southeast Asia, increasing the business and economic experience among the personnel it commits to the region, as well as shifting the focus of its attention politically. Normalizing relations with Vietnam would remove that nation as a special case in U.S. policy and release energies that could be used for much better purposes than arguing over what stands in the way of diplomatic relations. Reducing the official American establishment in the Philippines would make clear to the leaders of that nation that the special relationship is really over, and make possible more adequate representation elsewhere in the region. Public and private funding agencies need urgently to join forces to rescue the study of Southeast Asia in American universities, a field that is now an endangered species. The United States needs to do these things in order to pursue its own national interests more intelligently than it has done in the past or is doing now.

Chapter 4

The U.S. Economic Stake

The U.S. economic stake in Southeast Asia before the breakup of the Soviet Union was clear: the United States had an interest in the success of the market economies of its allies and friends in the region as part of its fight against communism. President Ronald Reagan was particularly active in expressing this view during his years in the White House. Following the collapse of the Soviet Union, this U.S. interest has not disappeared. It still matters to the United States that it has friends in a major world region like Southeast Asia who are following economic policies broadly similar to its own and making economic progress as a result. The difference now is that this is no longer part of a global ideological contest. In terms of economic policy, indeed, the government of Vietnam is busily reforming its economy to expand the operation of the market, and in Cambodia even Khmer Rouge leaders have conceded that "socialism is dead." What Americans want to know these days is, What are the economic benefits for the United States?

In these terms, the U.S. economic stake in Southeast Asia is large—much larger than many members of the U.S. policy community seem to realize. U.S. investments, about equally divided between oil and manufacturing, are significant in scale. American imports from Southeast Asia serve diverse domestic interests, including textiles, electronic components, and a broad range of consumer goods. But the outstanding element in the economic relationship between Southeast Asia and the United States is the record of U.S. exports. In 1992, 5 percent of U.S. exports went to Southeast Asia, compared with about 25 percent to the European Community. That is a very strong showing for a region that is just "taking off" economically or, in the case of its largest economy, is still developing. The United States now sells more each year to Southeast Asia than it sells to South America, to the Middle East, to Africa, or to all of the former Soviet Union and eastern Europe combined.

This is no accident. The open market of the United States was a major economic stimulus for Southeast Asia throughout the 1970s and 1980s. Now large portions of the population of the region for the first time are demanding goods and services of a kind that Americans take for granted. And they have steadily increasing disposable incomes that allow them to buy what Americans produce and have to sell.

The only serious problem in this picture lies in the fact that, as successful as U.S. exports have been, U.S. market shares are still not impressive. The U.S. share of the import market of these economies ranges from 11 percent to 20 percent, about the same as the European Community's; meanwhile, Japan and the combined economies of Korea, Taiwan, and Hong Kong have a higher share, notably in Indonesia, Malaysia, and Thailand. Why is the United States not doing better in such a favorable environment?

This is a crucial question, because what is happening in economic relations with Southeast Asia has implications for U.S. domestic and foreign economic policy as a whole. But for that to be understood clearly, it is necessary to understand the Southeast Asian economic landscape against which future U.S. policy will play out.

Southeast Asia has been a region of major economic winners and losers in recent decades. The losers have been the Indochina states of Vietnam, Cambodia, and Laos, plus Burma, all cases in which the ruling authorities have been committed to doctrines of economic management by command. The winners have been the ASEAN states of Indonesia, Thailand, Malaysia, and Singapore, all cases in which the national leadership has proceeded pragmatically in guiding mixed economies with large and growing modern private sectors. An additional, marginal member of the latter group has been the Philippines, where national political instability and imprudent economic policies have stalled growth for at least a decade.

The losers have become among the poorest economies in the world, in which prices became so artificial that they lost all meaning, and the World Bank and other international agencies became unable to make reliable estimates, even of how poor they had become. The winners have become among the most rapidly growing economies in the world. They have held to prudent monetary policies, and inflation has been kept under reasonable control. Savings and investment levels have been among the highest in the world. Economic output has been moving out of the production and export of primary commodities, which prevailed in the 1950s and 1960s, and into the production and export of manufactured goods. The average annual growth rates for the ASEAN economies were high from 1965 to 1980, ranging from almost 6 percent for the Philippines to 10 percent for Singapore (see Table 2). Growth rates were lower

TABLE 2—GROWTH OF PRODUCTION: SOUTHEAST ASIA

Country	GDP (millions of dollars)		Average annual growth of GDP (%)	
	1965	1990	1965–1980	1980–1990
Indonesia	5,980	107,290	7.0	5.5
Malaysia	3,130	42,400	7.4	5.2
Philippines	6,010	43,860	5.7	0.9
Singapore	970	34,600	10.0	6.4
Thailand	4,390	80,170	7.3	7.6
Burma	n.a.	n.a.	n.a.	n.a.
Cambodia	870	n.a.	n.a.	n.a.
Laos	n.a.	870	n.a.	n.a.
Vietnam	n.a.	n.a.	n.a.	n.a.

Source: World Bank, *World Development Report 1992* (New York: Oxford University Press, 1992), Tables 2 and 3.

n.a. = not available.

from 1980 to 1990, but except in the Philippines, they still ranged from 5 percent for Malaysia to almost 8 percent for Thailand. Estimates through 1994 have not varied from this picture; projected growth rates for Malaysia, Indonesia, Singapore, and Thailand are 6–8 percent. These remain high by world standards.[7]

For the Philippines, one effect of these high rates of growth among its neighbors has been the drastic relative decline of the domestic economy. In 1965 the Philippines had the largest economy in Southeast Asia. By 1990, Indonesia had the largest economy in the region, and Thailand had the second-largest. The Philippines had fallen to third place and was close to being overtaken by Malaysia and Singapore, both of which have much smaller populations.

This record of economic growth has been reinforced by the record of population growth. Between 1980 and 1990, the lowest population growth rates in the region, under 2 percent per annum, were recorded by Indonesia and Thailand (see Table 3); both governments had internationally acclaimed programs of family planning. Meanwhile, the highest rates, 2–3 percent, were reported for

TABLE 3—GROWTH OF POPULATION: SOUTHEAST ASIA

Country	Population (millions), 1990	Average annual growth of population (%)	
		1965–1980	1980–1990
Indonesia	178	2.4	1.8
Malaysia	18	2.5	2.6
Philippines	61	2.8	2.4
Singapore	3	1.6	2.2
Thailand	56	2.9	1.8
Burma	42	2.3	2.1
Cambodia	8	0.3	2.6
Laos	4	1.9	2.7
Vietnam	66	2.3	2.1

Source: World Bank, *World Development Report 1992* (New York: Oxford University Press, 1992), Table 26.

Malaysia, the Philippines, Cambodia, and Laos. These differentials have been enough to have a major impact on economic growth in per capita terms.

Estimates of gross national product (GNP) per capita in 1990, measured in U.S. dollars, reveal how the leading Southeast Asian countries have been coming up in the world (see Table 4). GNP per capita was higher in Singapore than in either Israel or Ireland, which means that Singapore was reaching into the lower range of western European income levels and, with virtually no foreign aid at all, had surpassed one of the principal recipients of American aid in the world. GNP per capita in Malaysia was well above that in Costa Rica or Chile, both commonly regarded as middle-class countries in Central and South America. Thailand's capita GNP was about equidistant between these of Colombia and Turkey, both among the

TABLE 4—GNP AND GDP PER CAPITA: SELECTED COUNTRIES

| Country | GNP per capita | | GDP per capita |
	Dollars, 1990	Average annual growth rate (%), 1965–1990	(Current international dollars), 1990
Singapore	11,160	6.5	14,920
Israel	10,920	2.6	11,940
Ireland	9,550	3.0	9,130
Malaysia	2,320	4.0	5,900
Chile	1,940	0.4	6,190
Costa Rica	1,900	1.4	4,870
Turkey	1,630	2.6	5,020
Thailand	1,420	4.4	4,610
Colombia	1,260	2.3	4,950
Dominican Republic	830	2.3	2,860
Philippines	730	1.3	2,320
Bolivia	630	− 0.7	1,910
Egypt	600	4.1	3,100
Indonesia	570	4.5	2,350

Source: World Bank, *World Development Report 1992* (New York: Oxford University Press, 1992), Tables 1 and 30.

more modern economies in their regions. The figure for the Philippines was, by comparison, equidistant between those for the Dominican Republic and Bolivia. And Indonesia, with minimal American aid, was about on a par with Egypt, which was the other leading recipient of American aid in the world. When GDP per capita is estimated in international dollars, which measure incomes in terms of their purchasing power in the domestic economy, Indonesia is seen to have moved marginally ahead of the Philippines.

What accounts for the pattern of losers and winners, the special case of the Philippines, and the significant differences among the other ASEAN economies?

Politics have mattered a great deal. It was crucial to the ASEAN economies that these states were anticommunist when the Cold War was swirling through the region. Indeed, they might be the only countries that benefited from the Vietnam War. Only Thailand and the Philippines had a security agreement with the United States. But Malaysia and Singapore had a similar agreement with the United Kingdom, Australia, and New Zealand. And Indonesia aligned itself with the United States from 1966 on. As a result, the economies of these countries looked to the United States and western Europe, which were the traditional markets for their exports, and toward Japan, Taiwan, and South Korea, the fastest-growing investors in the world.

Domestically, as well, politics have mattered. The ASEAN states other than the Philippines have had relatively stable political regimes during most of the time since 1965, and these regimes have tended to be led by politically conservative men who worked to retain existing political conditions and institutions. They have given a high priority to economic management, in part to justify their positions in offices of public authority in the absence of other grounds of legitimacy. Because of the authoritarian nature of their political regimes, they have been able to take a long-term view in economic decision-making. And policy has tended to be prudent, predictable, and very well prepared. The governments have been well served by relatively large numbers of senior policymakers trained in some of the best universities of the West.

Other factors also have been important. The region's strategic location encouraged generous economic assistance, from the United

States in the 1960s and early 1970s, and from Japan in the late 1970s and 1980s. World prices of tropical agricultural commodities were high throughout the 1970s. The oil price bonanzas of 1973 and 1979 helped Indonesia and Malaysia, although the volume was small relative to their populations, and their management of the bonanza was much better than most others'.[8]

The Philippines benefited less than the rest for several reasons. The nation was led for much of the period by Ferdinand Marcos, who destroyed the country's political institutions and manipulated its economic policies to serve short-term personal goals, often clothed in nationalist garb. The country was borrowing "just to maintain its lifestyle," as a secretary of finance put it. With the assassination of Benigno Aquino in 1983, billions of dollars fled the country; the hemorrhaging continued until 1993. Now that some stability has been restored, and the currency is freely convertible, the task is to break the monopolies and oligopolies that control so much of the country's banking and manufacturing. They have been protected by rules and tariffs that have kept competition out, savings low, and costs high, and have worked against Filipino exports and the Filipino consumer.

Each of the ASEAN countries has had its own pattern of growth. In Singapore, a welfare-minded government has managed the small urban economy meticulously; Singapore was the first nation in the region to court multinational corporations as investors and to seek a role in producing high-value-added goods for export. Malaysia, granting economic preferences to its indigenous Malay population following race riots in 1969, has created a larger public sector that has tended to slow the rate of growth somewhat. Thailand, early discarding import substitution and state ownership, has grown rapidly by giving free rein to its well-integrated Sino-Thai business community. Indonesia, which remained seriously under-developed into the early 1970s, has been the last to industrialize and to seek to export manufactured goods.

The domestic and international environments of these "ASEAN four"—Indonesia, Malaysia, Singapore, and Thailand—have been reflected in some of the highest savings and investment rates in the world. Gross domestic savings rates in 1990 were 45 percent in Singapore, 37 percent in Indonesia, 34 percent in Thai-

land, and 33 percent in Malaysia. Similarly, gross domestic investment rates in 1990 were 39 percent in Singapore, 37 percent in
Thailand, 36 percent in Indonesia, and 34 percent in Malaysia. The
comparable rates in the Philippines were 16 percent and 22 percent,
respectively. The world average for both savings and investments in
middle-income economies was 22 percent.[9]

Foreign investment also has been significant to the ASEAN
economies' growth. Net foreign investment in 1990, for example,
amounted to $2.9 billion in Malaysia, compared with $2.6 billion
in Mexico; $2.3 billion in Thailand, compared with $1.3 billion in
Brazil; $0.9 billion in Indonesia, compared with $0.5 billion in
Colombia; and $0.5 billion in the Philippines. Worldwide, few
countries of comparable size and development attracted higher
levels of investment.[10]

These investments have contributed to significant increases in
manufacturing in the ASEAN economies, and in manufactured
goods in their merchandise exports. All the economies except the
Philippines registered large increases in manufacturing between
1965 and 1990; each doubled the contribution of manufacturing to
its GDP in the twenty-five-year period (see Table 5). Manufactures

TABLE 5—ROLE OF MANUFACTURING: SOUTHEAST ASIA

Country	Manufacturing as % of GDP		Manufacturing as % of merchandise exports	
	1965	1990	1965	1990
Indonesia	8	20	4	35
Malaysia	9	28*	6	44
Philippines	20	25	6	62
Singapore	15	29	34	73
Thailand	14	26	3	64

Source: World Bank, *World Development Report 1992* (New York: Oxford University
Press, 1992), Tables 3 and 16; figure for Malaysia in 1991 is from U.S. National Committee
for Pacific Economic Cooperation, *Pacific Economic Outlook 1993–1994* (Washington,
D.C., 1993), p. 31.

*1991.

in 1990 amounted to 35 percent of exports from Indonesia and 44 percent from Malaysia, the two oil exporters among the ASEAN economies; and 73 percent from Singapore, 64 percent from Thailand, and 62 percent from the Philippines.

In sum, the economies of the ASEAN four have grown with extraordinary rapidity by world standards, fueled by substantial domestic and foreign investment, and guided by prudent macroeconomic policies. These developments have brought about a significant economic restructuring, away from the production and export of primary commodities, which prevailed in the 1950s and 1960s, and toward their replacement by the production and export of manufactures in the 1970s and 1980s. Restructuring also has occurred at the level of the regional economy, marked not only by the languishing of the former command economies, but also by the relative decline of the Philippine economy and the relative rise in prominence of Indonesia and Thailand.

IMPLICATIONS FOR U.S. INVESTMENT AND TRADE

The U.S. role in these rapidly changing economies is in part that of a source of direct investment. The total value of this investment in current market terms is not known.[11]

Southeast Asia is rich in deposits of petroleum and natural gas, and exploitation of these appears to be the largest object of U.S. investment in the region. Indonesia is the region's major producer of oil, and the world's largest producer of liquefied natural gas. These resources have attracted a large volume of U.S. investment to Indonesia. Some 60 percent of the foreign firms in the Indonesian oil industry are U.S. firms, and they reported total expenditures of $12.7 billion in Indonesia between 1980 and 1990; they had total sales of $5.4 billion in 1990 alone.[12] U.S. investment in the Indonesian oil and gas industry also appears likely to become even much larger; a vast reserve of natural gas off Natuna Island is to be developed by the Indonesian government and the Exxon Corporation at a cost estimated at $17 billion.[13]

Malaysia is the second-largest producer of oil and gas in the region, and it, too, has attracted substantial U.S. investment. U.S. oil firms were responsible for 65 percent of total U.S. assets of $7 billion in Malaysia in early 1992, or $4.5 billion. The same firms expect to invest another $3.1 billion in Malaysia by 1996.[14] Other recent finds of oil and gas deposits off the Philippines, Malaysia, Vietnam, and Hong Kong suggest that the region might be on its way to becoming a major producing region over the next decade.

Oil refining and related petrochemicals also have begun to bulk large in U.S. investments in Southeast Asia as economic growth has led to increased demands for energy, and as manufacturing has increased the demand for plastic feedstocks. Exxon is expanding its refining capacity in Thailand in a program that is costing more than $900 million. Mobil is completing a $635 million aromatics complex in Singapore, which will bring its total local investment to $1.6 billion.[15]

Thus U.S. investments in oil and natural gas production and in their downstream processing and marketing currently account, according to reports by U.S. firms operating in the region, for a total of almost $20 billion. Much of this amount is uncounted or undercounted in official investment data.

These two resources account for only a portion of existing U.S. investment in Southeast Asia. U.S. government data indicate that around 60 percent of total U.S. investment in the region might be in sectors other than oil and gas.[16] These include mining of hard minerals, manufacturing, and services, including banking and other financial services.

A notable case is the electrical and electronic goods industry. U.S. companies pioneered the development of this industry in Southeast Asia, beginning in the 1960s. They have helped make electronics the most important manufacturing industry of Singapore and Malaysia. The growth of these industries has spilled over into Thailand, where electronic products were the nation's leading export in 1991. They are to be differentiated, moreover, from the garment industry and other "footloose" industries that have been moving in recent decades from one low-wage economy to another. According to electronic industry representatives, low wages alone did not lure them to Southeast Asia in the first place. The primary attraction was the opportunity to operate in a free market environment with a well-educated work force able to speak English.[17] Over time the availability of engineers in the local population, often educated in the United States at the expense of their families, has become equally important as design functions and quality controls have been added to assembly operations in Southeast Asia. This has meant that U.S. producers of electronic systems for clients in western Europe can now have them designed and produced in Singapore or Malaysia and shipped directly from there.[18]

The United States has significant interests in trade with Southeast Asia, as well as in investments there. The ASEAN countries as a group constitute the largest regional trading partner of the United States after northeast Asia and the European Union. This has been the case every year since at least the mid-1980s. In 1990 U.S. two-way trade with the ASEAN economies, totaling $49.5 billion, was larger than U.S. trade with South America, with the Middle East, with Africa, or with the former Soviet Union and eastern Europe (see Table 6). U.S. exports of $20.6 billion were larger, as well.

The numbers are equally impressive in other respects. The United States sold $8.8 billion worth of merchandise to Singapore in 1991, more than it sold to China or to Saudi Arabia in the same year. The United States sold $3.9 billion worth of merchandise to Malaysia, more than it sold to Israel, one of the major recipients of U.S. foreign aid, or to the former Soviet Union. The U.S. sold $3.8 billion to Thailand, more than it sold to Egypt, another major recipient of U.S. foreign aid. Finally, the United States sold $1.9 billion to Indonesia, more than it sold to all of eastern Europe combined.

Not only are U.S. exports to the ASEAN economies large compared with exports to other regions, but they have been growing faster than exports to most other economies around the world because ASEAN per capita incomes have been rising faster than most others. This means that one way the U.S. economy can increase its own rate of growth is by increasing its exports to the ASEAN economies. Indeed, it is difficult to see how the United States can improve its global position without taking steps that will have this result. Leaders of firms at the high-technology end of U.S. manufacturing say their sales have already been growing faster in Thailand, for example, than in Japan.

U.S. exports to the ASEAN economies also are highly varied, which means that the profits are spread widely across the U.S.

TABLE 6—U.S. TRADE WITH SELECTED COUNTRIES (MILLIONS OF DOLLARS)
1991

Country or region	U.S. Exports	U.S. Imports	Total U.S. Trade
Indonesia	1,891	3,197	5,088
Malaysia	3,901	6,102	10,003
Philippines	2,269	3,471	5,740
Singapore	8,807	9,976	18,783
Thailand	3,757	6,125	9,882
ASEAN	20,625	28,871	49,496
China	6,287	18,976	25,263
Hong Kong	8,140	9,286	17,426
Taiwan	13,191	23,036	36,227
South Korea	15,518	17,025	32,543
South America	19,227	22,878	42,107
Saudi Arabia	6,572	10,978	17,550
Israel	3,858	3,497	7,355
Egypt	2,721	206	2,927
Middle East	15,275	15,868	31,143
Africa	6,713	12,484	19,197
USSR	3,577	813	4,390
Eastern Europe	1,208	997	2,205

Source: Office of Trade and Investment Analysis, International Trade Administration, U.S. Department of Commerce, *U.S. Foreign Trade Highlights 1991*, Tables 2 and 3.

economy. Apart from electronics components, the most prominent item in U.S. exports to every ASEAN economy is aircraft and associated equipment and parts. Other items amounting to more than $100 million in exports to one or more of the ASEAN economies in one recent year included data processing machines, engineering equipment, engines and motors, telecommunications equipment, electrical machinery, electrical apparatus for switching, musical tapes and records, tobacco, cotton, wheat, petroleum additives, and arms and ammunition.[19]

In short, U.S. investment in the ASEAN economies and U.S. trade with them have given the United States a substantial economic stake in Southeast Asia.

Chapter 5

Meeting the Japanese Challenge

Concern has arisen in American foreign policy circles that U.S. economic interests in Southeast Asia, important as they are, are being seriously eroded by competition from Japan. The belief is widespread that the Japanese are "taking over" the economies of Southeast Asia or, at the least, are acquiring a dominant position that threatens to reduce significantly the economic role of the United States. This belief has contributed to fears that a "yen trading bloc" is developing in greater East Asia, linking Japan with the economies of China, Taiwan, Hong Kong, and Southeast Asia.

This concern is as much an artifact of American worries about the general condition of the U.S. economy as it is reflective of developments in Southeast Asia. Pessimism about the ability of the United States to deal effectively with the deficits in its federal budget and its national balance of trade has been widespread in recent years. The 1992 presidential election demonstrated that the American voting public was deeply concerned about the ability of the American political system to grapple with such fundamental economic issues.

At the same time, studies by some American analysts put the future of the American economy squarely in terms of competition with Japan and Germany.[20] And Southeast Asia is seen as a principal arena of competition, for Japanese investments in the region exploded between 1985 and 1990. Japanese government data show that Japanese investment in the ASEAN economies was $706 million in 1985, $855 million in 1986, $1.5 billion in 1987, and $2.7 billion in 1988. The figure increased every year in every ASEAN economy. Singapore led with $302 million in 1986, Indonesia with $545 million in 1987, and Thailand with $859 million in 1988.[21] Thai government data show that approvals of Japanese investments peaked at $1.0 billion in 1990, then fell back to $674 million in 1991 and an estimated $497 million in 1992.[22]

This investment surge was not limited to investment in ASEAN. Japanese investment in Hong Kong also reached record levels in this period.[23] Japanese investment outflows to the world and to the rest of Asia did the same, before peaking in 1989.[24] In addition, the flow into Southeast Asia did not come only from Japan. Hong Kong and Singapore investment also was on the rise in Thailand, for example.[25] Nevertheless, the surge of Japanese investments in Thailand attracted particular attention. A U.S. trade official in Bangkok suggests that a "Chicken Little" phenomenon also was operating: so many members of the local U.S. chamber of commerce reported that the Japanese were "taking over" the Thai economy that many corporate executives in the United States came to believe it was so.

The surge of Japanese and other East Asian investment into Southeast Asia was followed by a rapid increase in ASEAN exports to the United States, particularly between 1991 and 1992. Total U.S. imports from the ASEAN economies went from $28.9 billion in 1991 to $36.1 billion in 1992 (see Table 7). Most of the increase came from Malaysia, Thailand, and Indonesia, all countries where, outside of the oil industry, the Japanese were by this time the leading foreign economic presence. China experienced the only increase that approached the ASEAN total; U.S. imports from China increased from $19.0 billion to $25.7 billion. During the same period, U.S. imports declined from South Korea and increased only modestly from Hong Kong and Taiwan. These changes lent credence to reports that manufacturing firms had been relocating from Japan, South Korea, Hong Kong, and Taiwan—to the ASEAN states and to China—in order to serve as export platforms aimed at the American market.

TABLE 7—U.S. IMPORTS FROM SELECTED EAST ASIAN AND PACIFIC
COUNTRIES (MILLIONS OF DOLLARS)

Country	1990	1991	1992
Brunei	95.7	26.5	29.5
Indonesia	3,341.2	3,240.5	4,566.5
Malaysia	5,271.8	6,101.5	8,293.7
Philippines	3,384.1	3,471.2	4,357.6
Singapore	9,800.4	9,956.3	11,317.5
Thailand	5,288.6	6,122.0	7,528.2
ASEAN Total	27,181.8	28,918.4	36,053.0
Australia	4,446.6	3,988.2	3,691.5
China	15,237.3	18,969.0	25,729.1
Hong Kong	9,621.6	9,278.5	9,799.2
Japan	89,684.1	91,510.6	97,181.4
South Korea	18,485.3	17,018.5	16,690.8
Taiwan	22,665.9	23,023.0	24,601.3
Other	2,090.7	1,132.9	2,188.7
East Asia and Pacific Total	189,413.3	194,666.0	215,953.2
World Total	495,310.5	488,055.4	532,497.7

Source: U.S. Department of Commerce, Bureau of the Census. Compiled by Gary Bouck, Office of the Pacific Basin.

Meanwhile, American exports to the ASEAN states did not experience anything like an increase on the same order, growing only from $20.8 billion in 1991 to $24.0 billion in 1992 (see Table 8). The result was to create a widening gap in the trade balance between the United States and the ASEAN states: the U.S. trade deficit with ASEAN went from $8.1 billion in 1991 to $12.1 billion in 1992 (see Table 9). This regional total was marked by particularly high U.S. trade deficits with Malaysia and Thailand—$3.9 billion and $3.6 billion, respectively. Among all the economies of East Asia and the Pacific in 1992, only Japan, China, and Taiwan surpassed these deficits. While only the deficits with Japan and China were substantially larger, at $49.4 billion and $18.3 billion, respectively, the United States was in deficit with every economy of any size in the region except Australia. And the U.S. trade deficit with the region was larger than the U.S. trade deficit with the world; U.S. trade

TABLE 8—U.S. EXPORTS TO SELECTED EAST ASIAN AND PACIFIC COUNTRIES
(MILLIONS OF DOLLARS)

Country	1990	1991	1992
Brunei	142.8	162.3	453.0
Indonesia	1,897.2	1,891.5	2,777.8
Malaysia	3,425.0	3,899.9	4,395.8
Philippines	2,470.7	2,264.9	2,753.1
Singapore	8,022.6	8,803.8	9,623.6
Thailand	2,955.3	3,752.7	3,982.3
ASEAN Total	18,953.6	20,775.1	23,985.6
Australia	8,537.7	8,403.9	8,912.6
China	4,806.4	6,278.3	7,469.6
Hong Kong	6,816.7	8,137.1	9,068.6
Japan	48,579.6	48,125.3	43,763.9
South Korea	14,404.1	15,504.9	14,630.1
Taiwan	11,490.8	13,182.4	15,204.7
Other	1,467.2	1,443.1	1,853.9
East Asia and Pacific Total	115,056.1	121,850.1	128,889.0
World Total	393,592.3	421,730.0	448,156.3

Source: U.S. Department of Commerce, Bureau of the Census. Compiled by Gary Bouck, Office of the Pacific Basin.

outside of East Asia and the Pacific was more or less in balance. The part of the world that the United States has to do something about in order to reduce or eliminate its trade deficit is East Asia. And increasingly that includes the ASEAN economies.

A Japanese analyst has attributed the surge of Japanese investment to Southeast Asia to three factors: yen appreciation, economic friction with the United States and the European Community, and a blue-collar worker shortage in Japan.[26] The yen appreciation resulted primarily from the so-called Plaza Accord of 1985. In September of that year, meeting at the Plaza Hotel in New York, the ministers of finance of the Group of 5 (the United States, Japan, West Germany, the United Kingdom, and France) agreed to the devaluation of the U.S. dollar, especially in relation to the Japanese yen and German mark, in order to strengthen U.S. export competitiveness and reduce the continuing U.S. trade deficit. Subsequent

TABLE 9—U.S. TRADE BALANCE WITH SELECTED EAST ASIAN AND PACIFIC
COUNTRIES (MILLIONS OF DOLLARS)

Country	1990	1991	1992
Brunei	47.1	135.8	423.5
Indonesia	(1,444.0)	(1,346.0)	(1,748.7)
Malaysia	(1,846.8)	(2,201.6)	(3,897.9)
Philippines	(913.4)	(1,206.3)	(1,604.5)
Singapore	(1,777.8)	(1,152.9)	(1,693.9)
Thailand	(2,293.3)	(2,369.3)	(3,545.9)
ASEAN Total	(8,228.2)	(8,143.3)	(12,067.4)
Australia	4,091.1	4,415.7	5,221.1
China	(10,430.9)	(12,690.7)	(18,259.5)
Hong Kong	(2,804.9)	(1,141.4)	(730.6)
Japan	(41,104.5)	(43,385.3)	(49,417.5)
South Korea	(4,081.2)	(1,513.6)	(2,060.7)
Taiwan	(11,175.1)	(9,840.6)	(9,396.6)
Other	(623.5)	(516.7)	(335.0)
East Asia and Pacific Total	(74,357.2)	(72,815.9)	(87,047.1)
World Total	(101,718.2)	(65,399.0)	(84,341.4)

Source: U.S. Department of Commerce, Bureau of the Census. Compiled by Gary Bouck,
Office of the Pacific Basin.

pressure from the United States led the governments of South Korea
and Taiwan to realign their currencies more or less in harmony with
the new value of the yen. During the latter half of the 1980s much
else beyond the Plaza Accord was occurring that alarmed Japanese
manufacturers. Many of the same pressures that led to calls for
currency realignment also led to more assertive American trade
policies. Prominent among these was the U.S. Trade Act of 1988,
which strengthened the ability of the U.S. government to retaliate
unilaterally against foreign practices perceived as detrimental to
U.S. commercial interests. Also, in February 1988 a Bank of Japan
survey found more industries reporting a shortage of labor than
reporting the traditional surplus.[27]

As the stronger yen and these other factors led to a surge of
foreign investment by Japanese firms, much of it was oriented to the
ASEAN region. In 1987, almost 20 percent of Japan's overseas

investment was in "developing" East Asia, including ASEAN, compared with only 6 percent of U.S. investment.[28] And 60 percent of the Japanese investment in "developing" East Asia was in the ASEAN countries. Japanese manufacturers in these countries reported in 1989 that they had invested there principally because of the low-cost labor, but also to cultivate the local market.[29] So there was ample experience among Japanese manufacturing industries to lead them to step up their investment in the ASEAN region in the late 1980s.

The government of Japan had a major role in facilitating the surge of Japanese investment. The Overseas Economic Cooperation Fund (OECF) of Japan, one of the most powerful national aid agencies in the world, was a principal player. In 1989 the OECF managed some 58 percent of Japan's bilateral foreign aid, which was chiefly in the form of loans made on a concessional basis to the governments of developing countries. More than 77 percent of the OECF's loan commitments were to Asian, mainly Southeast Asian, governments. And in three ASEAN countries—Indonesia, the Philippines, and Thailand—the OECF was in 1988 the top donor among governments and intergovernmental institutions, including the World Bank and the Asian Development Bank.[30] A much debated issue is the extent to which Japanese aid is associated with private Japanese industrial interests.[31]

Less well known than its role as an aid agency is the fact that the OECF also finances loans to and equity investment in private corporations registered in Japan and corporations in developing countries that are associated with Japanese interests. The OECF has equity investment in several types of intermediary investment corporations, including the Japan ASEAN Investment Company. This entity was founded in 1981 with 137 member corporations of the Japan Association of Corporate Executives as shareholders. A series of expansions brought the funds of the ASEAN Investment Company to 71.6 billion yen between its founding in 1981 and 1990–1991, by which time it had invested in 50 ASEAN corporations.[32]

The Export-Import Bank of Japan also played a significant role in the Japanese investment surge. Under 1986 legislation, the role of the Export-Import Bank was changed from promoting exports to encouraging Japanese foreign investment. The bank began to extend credits to Japanese firms to provide them with funds for investment abroad. The credits were usable for equity participation in foreign corporations as well as for long-term loans. By 1990, export credits amounted to only 12 percent of Ex-Im Bank financing. The share of overseas investment credits rose to 37 percent.[33]

In addition, Japan's Ministry for International Trade and Industry established in 1987 a new insurance system that provided protection against losses by Japanese corporations supplying plants and capital equipment to overseas subsidiaries and joint ventures. The system specifically provided protection to small and medium-scale manufacturers that established production facilities abroad for exporting products to third countries.[34]

The ASEAN governments were well aware of their increased international competitiveness vis-à-vis Japan, Taiwan, and South Korea as a result of the currency realignment of 1985. Also, they were under considerable pressure to take advantage of the new situation created by the global recession, which reached Southeast Asia in 1985–1986, drying up savings, investment, and exports, and causing severe balance-of-payments deficits. The recession was particularly severe in Singapore, but it was a major source of pressure for policy change in the other countries, as well. Where foreign investment was heavily regulated, as in Malaysia and Indonesia, the external environment provided an opportunity for policy reformers to press to deregulate investment and trade regimes substantially. Where controls were already minimal, as in Singapore, the government reduced the cost of doing business by cutting taxes, public service fees, and labor benefits. Where conditions were midway between these, as in Thailand, the government did some of each. All four countries offered special incentives to investors who would come in to build factories that would export the bulk of their production.[35]

Government policy preferences also operated in the ASEAN states in other respects. The Singapore government's long-term strategy was to rely on foreign investment in high-technology and high-value-added industries and services, such as electronics, avionics, biotechnology, and computer software. Malaysia's long-term aim was to industrialize as part of its Look East policy, which favored Japanese and Korean firms in order to promote the emulation of their work habits; the program included free trade zones where materials and components were imported, processed, or assembled, and then reexported. Thailand continued to look to its private sector as the primary engine of growth, and the private sector continued to seek its comparative advantages in tourism and in the export, principally to the United States, of textiles, garments, and electronics. Indonesia was unable to sustain its preferred program of state-owned industrial expansion, and the private sector there followed that of Thailand in large measure.

The surge of Japanese investment into Southeast Asia was thus a result of long-term and short-term market forces and policy responses by the governments of Japan and the ASEAN states. The currency realignment of 1985 and Japan's trade frictions with the United States and western Europe seemed likely to be of enduring consequence. At the same time, the adjustment by Japanese industry to the currency realignment appeared to have been accomplished by the early 1990s, and by this time, Tokyo had other priorities. The collapse of the "bubble economy" of the late 1980s in Japan gave the government the new priority of reinvigorating the economy at home. Abroad, the Japanese government faced multiple pressures to finance economic development elsewhere than in Southeast Asia—in China, in eastern Europe, and in the former Soviet Union. Meanwhile, in Southeast Asia, the ASEAN economies were now in competition for Japanese funds with Vietnam and Cambodia.

Thus, a real and powerful surge of foreign direct investment in Southeast Asia took place in the last half of the 1980s. Not all of this investment came from Japan; the surge included investment from elsewhere, as well. And Southeast Asia was not the only recipient; China also experienced a surge of foreign direct investment, principally from Hong Kong, Taiwan, and Chinese communities in Southeast Asia. But Japan had a great deal to do with the Southeast Asian experience, and was left in a stronger position in the ASEAN economies than ever before. Speaking in Bangkok in January 1993, Prime Minister Miyazawa said that Japanese direct investment in the ASEAN economies since the Plaza Accord of 1985 amounted to roughly $20 billion, and exports of manufactured products from the ASEAN countries to Japan had increased 4.6 times between 1986 and 1991.[36]

EXPORT EXPANSION AS A POLICY RESPONSE

These events are not, on their face, contrary to the interests of the United States. A strong Japanese economic presence in Southeast Asia has long been a given among American economists, in view of the physical proximity of the two and in view of their comparative advantages. Japan is a natural source of capital and technology for Southeast Asia, and Southeast Asia is a natural source of raw materials and markets for the industry of Japan. Moreover, let us make no mistake about it: Japanese investment has filled a large place in the economies of Southeast Asia that American investors have left vacant by default.

But the level of American concern is rising, and not only because of the American economic pessimism of recent years. One cause of concern is the well-founded perception that Japanese and other East Asian manufacturers are transferring their operations to third countries in Southeast Asia principally as a means of escaping currency and trade accords, and so are continuing, with the support of their governments, to contribute to the U.S. trade deficit. Another is that the growing economic ties between Japanese corporate interests and Southeast Asian government bureaucracies are resulting in increasing numbers of cases in which American firms are frozen out of major government procurement contracts for reasons that have little to do with quality or prices.

There is no escaping the fact that, at the same time that the United States and Japan are cooperating in Southeast Asia in important ways, they are competing head-to-head to convert economic opportunities into economic benefits. The question is, What can Americans learn from recent experience that will enable the United States to compete more effectively in the future?

The most important step the United States needs to take to promote its economic interests in Southeast Asia is to start giving priority attention to its export opportunities. If the Clinton administration pursues that policy, it will have multiple implications. It will mean less official reliance on legal approaches to trade and more recourse to financial ones. It also will mean less reliance on uni-lateral threats and sanctions, and more recourse to bilateral and multilateral remedies. Some of the needed policy changes can be accomplished fairly quickly, but others will require time. The argu-ment for change, whether short-term or long-term, is necessarily global. But recent U.S. experience in Southeast Asia provides some potent ammunition.

Let us be clear about the recent past. It has been wrong for other governments to close their eyes to the practices of local firms in copying patented American pharmaceuticals, and copyrighted American video and music tapes, without a by-your-leave from the Americans who created these materials. It has been right for the U.S. Trade Representative to campaign vigorously to move foreign gov-ernments to honor the intellectual property rights of American firms and individuals. But let us also be frank about the dynamics of the situation. Intellectual property rights are not the only issues in which the United States has an economic interest, and they are not necessarily the most lucrative ones for the U.S. economy. The big-gest economic opportunities lie in the new infrastructure projects that rapid growth is obliging the governments of Southeast Asia to build—oil refineries, power plants, transport systems, telecom-munications systems—all things that American manufacturers are in a good position to provide. The U.S. Trade Act of 1988 has diverted official U.S. attention from these opportunities.

How the United States managed its economic relations with Thailand in recent years offers a leading example of this point. In 1989, in accordance with the U.S. Trade Act of 1988, Washington cited Thailand for not providing adequate protection for intellectual property; in fact Thailand was notorious for its pirating of Western trademarks. A year later, the U.S. entertainment and pharmaceuti-cal industries filed suits with the U.S. Trade Representative. In 1991 Thailand was designated a "priority foreign country" under the "special 301" provisions of the Trade Act, and sanctions were in the offing. There was a burst of activity in Bangkok to comply with the U.S. demands. In addition, as it happened, the prime minister of Thailand was personally acquainted with U.S. President George Bush; they had been ambassadors to the United Nations together earlier in their careers. The prime minister flew to Washington to see his old friend. Meanwhile, concern was reported from Bangkok that the Thai military might use trade tensions to put off national elections, a matter about which the U.S. president had written the Thai prime minister with warm encouragement. As a result, by the end of 1991 President Bush decided that Thailand was making a genuine effort to protect intellectual property, and the crisis passed. Even so, in 1992 the U.S. Trade Representative reported that Thai performance was still unsatisfactory. Evidently the United States had not yet found a satisfactory means for handling such disputes.

Thai and American trade officials in Bangkok seemed to be in agreement about one point. The intellectual property rights in dispute, significant as they were, were of much less value to the U.S. economy than the export opportunities in fields in which Thailand was becoming a major buyer. A Thai trade official estimated that $500 million was involved in the intellectual property dispute, while $2 billion was involved in current opportunities in telecommunications alone.[37] According to a U.S. trade official, the dispute over intellectual property rights "isn't important to the U.S. in the overall scheme of things [and] isn't important to the Thais either."[38]

An area of contention among such officials has been whether U.S. firms are able to make sales and investments on a basis of equality with other firms. For example, at the peak of the intellectual property rights dispute, in September 1991, an American company lost out to a Taiwan competitor for a $300 million petrochemical investment opportunity in Thailand. A Thai official said the American proposal was not competitive in its financing. "There has been case after case of Americans losing out in competitive bidding because they do not have competitive financing," he said.[39] A U.S. official saw it differently. The Taiwan firm had "lowballed" the Thai Board of Investment, beaten out the American firm, and then come back a year later to renegotiate terms. But the U.S. government was in disarray on the foreign economic policy front. "No one seems to have any idea," the U.S. official said, "of what it means to 'support American business.' "[40]

The first lesson the Thai experience can offer is that unilateral threats of economic sanctions on the part of the U.S. government do work. Under threat of U.S. sanctions, the Thai legislature amended the trademark law to provide what the U.S. Trade Representative described as "substantially improved trademark protection," and amended the patent law to extend protection to pharmaceuticals; meanwhile, the Thai government also pledged to increase its enforcement efforts on copyrights.[41] Unilateral threats of sanctions are likely to remain for some time.

Still, disputes over intellectual property probably would not bulk so large if U.S. relations were progressing more positively on other fronts. Significantly, of all the economies of Southeast Asia, Thailand had the largest trade surplus with the United States in 1990 and 1991. That surplus—around $2.3 billion each year—was not large by East Asian standards, but it made Thailand stand out in Southeast Asia and increased the U.S. government's leverage on the Thai government. Then, in February 1991 the Thai military staged a coup and brought down the government of an elected prime minister. After that there was no sympathy left for Thailand anywhere in Washington. The second lesson: Governments that want to avoid U.S. sanctions should watch their trade balances and keep their armed forces under control.

The principal alternative the United States has to reducing imports by way of sanctions and other forms of protection is to increase its exports. Increasing U.S. exports to match the rise in exports of Thailand and other countries in East and Southeast Asia should be a high priority, but it seems to be unusually difficult. The United States has gotten its trade with most of the world in balance since 1985, but U.S. trade is in deficit with almost every economy of East and Southeast Asia. Many U.S. officials concerned with this trade believe that American firms are simply not export-oriented enough to compete in this part of the world. Some U.S. companies, such as Motorola, Bechtel, and Boeing, get high marks; American firms are competitive when they want to be. But U.S. officials believe that U.S. business is largely concerned with other things. In the words of a U.S. Export-Import Bank official in Washington, promoting U.S. exports to Thailand "is like pushing on a string."[42] As a U.S. trade official in Bangkok expressed it, "There is just no constituency for foreign trade."[43] New incentives are needed to change traditional corporate behavior.

Increasing U.S. exports also is tied to increasing U.S. investment abroad; nearly 30 percent of all U.S. exports go to overseas subsidiaries and affiliates of American firms. Yet no one is optimistic about the prospect that the United States will be able to increase its investments abroad on any appreciable scale at any time soon. In the words of one former investment banker, now a senior economic official in the Clinton administration, "It is almost impossible to stress enough the poor position that the United States is in to make investments in Southeast Asia or elsewhere abroad relative to Japan. . . . If you look at the requirements [here at home], you have to conclude that there will be a ten-year period, at least, in which capital outflows from the United States in any significant amount—and certainly relative to the capital surplus countries in Asia—will be extremely minimal."[44] While we are thus dealing here with a long-term goal, it is one that carries the highest possible priority. As President Clinton has been arguing, the United States must stop living beyond its means. It is strategically important that the United States become a nation of savers and investors again.

At the same time, the bulk of U.S. exports is not tied to investment abroad, and there is ample scope for export expansion. Indeed, it is difficult to see how the U.S. economy can grow at a faster rate without export expansion, especially to East and Southeast Asia, because these economies are growing so much faster than our own. The question that arises is if exports are not a high priority from the vantage point of many U.S. private firms, but are a high priority for the U.S. economy as a whole, what can Washington do to increase the incentives for U.S. firms to engage in the export trade?

The principal step the U.S. government needs to take is to get its own house in order. The appointment of an advisor to the president on all domestic and foreign economic policy has been a significant first step. But the United States urgently needs to overhaul the management of foreign economic policy all the way down the line. U.S. diplomatic personnel in Southeast Asia are scathing in their criticism of the situation in Washington. So many agencies are involved in foreign economic policy, one ambassador said, "I would have to be the chief executive officer of a big multinational corporation with my own lobbyists in Washington to know whom to contact about any particular problem or opportunity."[45] A high priority is increasing the professional quality of the Department of

Commerce and its numerous dependent agencies, which are said to be among the most heavily staffed by political appointees of any in the U.S. government. Another priority is increasing rapidly the appointment to the Department of State of men and women with economic training and commercial experience, and retraining other U.S. diplomatic personnel with an eye to the new economic missions they are expected to perform. One of the most useful early steps would be to staff and finance more adequately the U.S. and Foreign Commercial Service, which is the main instrument through which the U.S. government helps private U.S. business firms, especially smaller and middle-size ones that cannot afford their own offices abroad, with the information and advice they need to take advantage of export opportunities.

Washington also should move quickly to mobilize U.S. financial institutions to support U.S. exports. To return to the Thai case, Bangkok is planning a large number of major infrastructure projects, including electric power generating plants, oil refineries, water treatment systems, urban rail transit systems, telephone systems, a new international airport, and natural gas pipelines. These projects are worth tens of billions of dollars, and a large part of their budgets will go to pay for foreign-made machinery and material. According to American trade officials in Bangkok, U.S. manufacturers are well qualified to respond to these opportunities, but the U.S. private financial sector is not, and U.S. public financial agencies do not have enough lending authority to cover them all.[46] The prime U.S. financing facility, the U.S. Export-Import Bank, already faces current requests for up to $1.5 billion in project financing, a sum that would quadruple its exposure in Thailand.[47] The scope for improvement in matching major export sales opportunities with U.S. public and private financing is considerable.

The U.S. Congress should promptly support the National Export Strategy, which President Clinton announced in September 1993. U.S. export credits are notorious for their current bias in favor of agriculture; the secretary of commerce has reported that 80 percent of U.S. export promotion dollars are spent on agricultural products, although they represent only 10 percent of U.S. exports. U.S. exports of manufactured goods and the U.S. jobs in manufacturing that they represent depend on financing that is competitive. It makes every kind of sense to approve an expansion of Export-Import Bank funds immediately. It also is eminently reasonable to open offices around the United States to make it possible for the owners and operators of small businesses, who cannot afford to have a representative in Washington, and who have yet to learn to navigate the electronic information system of the Commerce Department, to obtain information about export opportunities and help in applying for federal export financing. The argument that the U.S. government has spent years trying to limit such export subsidies on the part of other governments is in fact an argument in favor of the subsidies. U.S. preaching has had little or no effect in the past. With a strong export promotion program of its own, the United States will be in a stronger position to negotiate with its competitors in East Asia.[48]

A decade ago, Lawrence Krause, a leading American student of Pacific trade, argued that what was needed to promote U.S. economic interests in Southeast Asia was a new relationship between the U.S. government and American business.[49] That new relationship remains equally needed today.

THE ISSUE OF A REGIONAL TRADE BLOC

At the same time, the United States must protect its economic interests from the possible growth of a regional trade bloc in East and Southeast Asia. The possibility exists for two reasons. One is that regional bias has been developing in the trade of these states, meaning that they are trading increasingly with each other and thus increasing the bonds of interest that unite them. The other reason is that, as many in East and Southeast Asia fear, the United States might act to protect its own manufacturing industry in ways that will reduce their access to U.S. markets. For both reasons, a community of economic interest has been growing that has variously been identified as a "trade bloc," an "economic group," and an "economic caucus." Whatever it is called, the possibility is an association among the economies of East and Southeast Asia, centered on Japan, the world's second-largest economy, and intent on negotiating with the United States from a position of strength.

No U.S. official is likely to view such a prospect with equanimity. In 1992 the House Committee on Ways and Means asked the U.S. International Trade Commission to investigate the causes and implications for the United States of economic integration in East Asia. While the experts the commission consulted varied in their opinions, many saw economic integration arising from a combination of macroeconomic forces, strategic business decisions, government policies, political relations, and other factors, and saw the process as likely to continue. And while most did not believe an exclusionary economic bloc was likely to form in the region, there was an important caveat: If the Uruguay Round of talks under the aegis of the General Agreement on Tariffs and Trade (GATT) were to fail, or if the United States continues to concentrate on the North American Free Trade Agreement (NAFTA) and on expanding negotiations to Latin America, the nations of East Asia might try to form a regional economic association as a second-best alternative.[50]

There is reason to question the viability of any such effort, but first it will be useful to examine the concerns about GATT and NAFTA, as these have some political potency, not only in Japan, but also in Southeast Asia.

The principal concern in Southeast Asia has been with the Uruguay Round of GATT negotiations. The regional economies are increasingly reliant on trade, and they are trading globally. Most are agricultural exporters, and they would benefit from easier access to the agricultural markets of the United States and western Europe. Most also are exporters of textiles and garments, and they would benefit from the phasing out of the restrictive quotas of the Multi-Fiber Agreement. In return, the Southeast Asian economies would benefit from an expansion of U.S. service industries in their economies, currently limited by politically influential local interests. It was particularly frustrating for the governments of Southeast Asia when the Uruguay Round had stalled, because they were effectively unrepresented in the negotiations. The economies of North America, western Europe, and Japan are so large, and are of such import for each other, that the talks inevitably centered on these in the end, and the governments of countries with smaller economies were able to do little but sit on the sidelines and watch. The situation was particularly galling for the government of Indonesia, with the fourth-largest population in the world and the leadership of the nonaligned movement in its hands. The Indonesians launched a highly public campaign to obtain an invitation for President Soeharto to the July 1993 meeting of the Group of 7, the major industrial powers, but had to be content with meetings with individual leaders in place of a role in the main event. The conclusion of the Uruguay Round in November 1993 is beneficial economically to the states of Southeast Asia and should go a long way toward clearing the air politically.

NAFTA also has been of serious concern to Southeast Asia. The initial agreement between the United States and Canada did not attract much attention in Southeast Asia, because the Canadian economy was only marginally competitive with the economies of Southeast Asia in the U.S. market. The addition of Mexico has been a different matter. Policymakers in Southeast Asia understand that Mexico is of strategic interest to the United States—that the United States has an opportunity to stem the tide of Mexican migration by helping reduce poverty in Mexico. At the same time, many economists in Southeast Asia see expansion of NAFTA to include Mexico as likely to divert from their economies investment aimed at production for the U.S. market. Mexico not only has the advantage of relatively short distances to U.S. markets; it also has wage levels comparable to those of Southeast Asia. The extension of NAFTA to Mexico also was troubling to Southeast Asians because it raised questions about where U.S. trade policy was heading. The Bush administration was the proponent of a vigorous "Americas first" approach to foreign trade.

In June 1990 President Bush announced the Enterprise for the Americas initiative, saying he looked forward to the day when "all are equal partners in a free-trade zone stretching from the port of Anchorage to the Tierra del Fuego." Within a year, the United States had signed bilateral "framework" agreements, a first step toward free trade negotiations, with Chile, Colombia, Costa Rica, Ecuador, El Salvador, Honduras, Nicaragua, Panama, Peru, and Venezuela.[51] A senior Bush administration official said privately that the Enterprise proposal was aimed at shocking the Europeans and Japanese into making concessions in the GATT negotiations. If so, it did not have that effect. Instead, for many in East and Southeast Asia, it gave a sense of reality to what had previously been only a formless fear—that a "fortress America" mentality was developing at the peak of American politics, and that they were among the likely victims.

As we have seen, the economies of Southeast Asia have been growing much faster than those of Central and South America. And U.S. sales to the ASEAN economies have been more valuable to the United States than its sales to the Americas beyond Canada and Mexico. It therefore makes no economic sense for the United States to tie itself to the sluggish and ill-managed economies of Central and South America through a series of new trade agreements, and separate itself in the process from the dynamic and well-managed economies of Southeast Asia. Nothing the United States could do in the coming years would more surely advance the emergence of three inward-looking trading blocs in the global economy. It is not even clear that a further expansion of free trade agreements in any direction is necessarily in the interest of the United States. The United States should wait until the effects of free trade with Mexico are known before plunging ahead with expansion to additional countries. More thought certainly should go to the issue of sequencing, to the order in which, nation by nation, the United States should agree to additions to NAFTA.

The Enterprise initiative sent a call to arms through East and Southeast Asia. In 1991 Malaysian Prime Minister Datuk Scri Mahathir Mohamad proposed that Japan lead a new group, the East Asian Economic Grouping (EAEG), which expressly excluded the United States. Prime Minister Mahathir was already well known as the originator of Malaysia's Look East policy, which urged Malaysians to emulate the discipline of the Japanese. He also has been a frequent critic of Western liberalism on the grounds that it has promoted, in the name of human rights, public immorality and disorder. Faced with the prospect of a single European market and NAFTA, the Malaysian leader was widely understood to be proposing an East Asian trade bloc. Washington opposed the Malaysian proposal with unusual vigor—so much so that other Asian governments felt obliged to come to Prime Minister Mahathir's nominal defense. The fear was that if Malaysia's neighbors did not enable him to "save face," Malaysia might obstruct the carefully worked-out entry of ASEAN into the Asia Pacific Economic Cooperation organization (about which more shortly). The controversy over the proposed EAEG continued.

ASEAN economic ministers meeting in Kuala Lumpur in October 1991 agreed to a watered-down version of the Mahathir proposal, known as the East Asian Economic Caucus (EAEC). Membership would be on invitation by the ASEAN governments, and the caucus would meet on an ad hoc basis, as and when the need arose. The United States was not mollified. Secretary of State James Baker wrote Japanese Foreign Minister Michio Watanabe that the EAEC would "divide the Pacific region in half" and asked Japan not to participate. Secretary Baker also put strong pressure on the government of South Korea to oppose the caucus.[52]

Nevertheless, Tokyo reportedly was ready to "tolerate" the caucus idea "for the time being."[53] And Saburo Okita, who planned the postwar renaissance of the Japanese economy, was a founder of the Pacific Community movement, and had served as his country's foreign minister, wrote approvingly of the idea. "The EAEC concept was clearly formulated within a context of concern that Asia would be the loser as Europe and North America rushed to establish their own economic blocs," he wrote in the *Japan Times*. "Accordingly, the EAEC will probably have less impact if the [European Community] and NAFTA move clearly and decisively to reject discriminatory measures that would impact the East Asian economies adversely."[54]

With the United States opposed, the caucus idea was put on a back burner, but it is not dead by any means. Many in Japan and Southeast Asia view it as an "insurance policy" that they can fall back on if the new trade agreements of western Europe and North America prove to be unduly protective. Yet the initial Baker reaction was well founded—the EAEG or EAEC could divide the Pacific right down the middle. And that possibility contains a capacity for damage that could not be in the interest of anyone involved—not Southeast Asia, not Japan, and not the United States.

The obstacles to an East Asian economic bloc are several. All the potential members have experienced growing trade among themselves, but more because of differences in their resources and levels of development than because of common ground. All have the United States as a major export market—for most it is *the* major export market—but they do not all have an interest in the same sectors of the U.S. market. There are obstacles to Japanese leadership of an economic bloc, as well, including the weakness of its coalition government, dangers to Japan of risking a break with the United States, and Japan's continuing inability to provide its Asian trading partners with adequate access to its markets. And there are obstacles to followership among Asian peoples who experienced Japanese military occupation during the 1930s and 1940s. Followers might be particularly difficult to attract in China, Hong Kong, and Taiwan, whose economic relations with each other have been a major force for growth in the early 1990s. In addition, new ways of measuring China's GDP, putting it on a par with Germany, are not likely to lessen China's ambitions to regional leadership.

Meanwhile an alternate vision of the economic future of East Asia and the Pacific—one that *includes* the United States—also is taking shape. In late 1989, at a meeting in Canberra, representatives of the ASEAN states and their "dialogue partners"—the United States, Japan, Canada, Australia, New Zealand, and South Korea— founded an intergovernmental body under the name of Asia Pacific Economic Cooperation (APEC). It was the first time that governments of the Asia-Pacific region as a whole decided to create an association among themselves. The senior U.S. representative present called the event "a milestone in Pacific Basin cooperation." Foreign Minister Ali Alatas of Indonesia was perhaps nearer to the mark when he said that while there were "impediments and pitfalls that still stand in the way of efforts to transform lofty aspirations into solid achievements," the decision to create the new organization "might well prove to be a watershed."[55]

By the time the group met in Seoul in November 1991, the membership had been expanded to include China, Taiwan, and Hong Kong, for a total of fifteen entities. And by September 1992, the members had agreed to set up a small permanent secretariat in Singapore. For now APEC is a loosely structured forum. An Eminent Persons Group of eleven, drawn from as many countries, has made recommendations looking toward such possibilities as a Pacific common market and a Pacific free trade agreement. But these lie far in the future. For the near term, the prospect is that APEC will be more significant politically than economically.

Australia, the first proponent of APEC, had been pressing for a summit meeting of the heads of state of all fifteen members.[56] President Clinton was quick to grasp the opportunity to propose an informal gathering of Asia-Pacific political leaders at an APEC ministerial meeting set for Seattle in November 1993. It was a spectacular initiative. Such a meeting was unprecedented. And many Pacific leaders were known to be concerned by what they considered Washington's inattention to Asian affairs. At the same time, the lack of prior consultation by the United States and the prospect of the historic event's taking place in North America rather than in Asia dampened the initial enthusiasm. Nevertheless, Malaysia Prime Minister Mahathir was the sole holdout. The conference was expected to give APEC a strong boost. And the effort to reengage the United States in Asia-Pacific affairs had taken a giant step.

For the ASEAN states, entry into APEC signified a reluctant recognition of their limitations in the arena of economic diplomacy. The decision was closely argued among the ASEAN governments. On the one hand, they feared that ASEAN would lose some of its separate identity if they became members of the larger organization. On the other hand, they concluded that the ASEAN economies together were not large enough to provide a sufficient base for representing their interests effectively. Hence the guarded decision to go along with APEC.

The ASEAN decision to enter APEC had a significant outcome for its economic diplomacy with the United States, for it slowed the impetus behind efforts to nurture a special ASEAN–U.S. economic relationship. The U.S. Trade Representative in the first Reagan administration, William Brock, had believed that the economies of ASEAN and the United States were more complementary than competitive; he had argued that it was reasonable to expect these economies to grow closer over time. The idea was taken up in the late 1980s in a study sponsored by the Institute of Southeast Asian Studies in Singapore and the East-West Center in Honolulu. The scholars proposed an "ASEAN–U.S. initiative," to take the form of an umbrella agreement under which the ASEAN and U.S. governments would establish guidelines for negotiations on a wide range of issues, including subsidies, double taxation, intellectual property rights, investment rules, services, and nontariff barriers.[57] Their efforts led to the signing in late 1990 of a memorandum of under-standing by representatives of the ASEAN and U.S. governments. The agreement established a trade and investment cooperation committee aimed at monitoring and reviewing trade and investment relations, identifying opportunities for expanding them, and hold-ing regular consultations on trade and investment issues.

With the end of the Cold War, however, there was little or no political commitment to this initiative. U.S. attention was directed elsewhere. By early 1993, it was possible for a prominent ASEAN policy analyst, long identified with the United States, to say that he welcomed the Clinton presidency, including its likely attention to human rights, "because that is more attractive than no attention at all."[58] This was a considerable retreat from the days of the Reagan presidency. And by now the ASEAN initiative was overshadowed by the EAEC dispute and by the development of APEC.

On short acquaintance, the ASEAN Free Trade Area (AFTA) seems unlikely to change the general prospect. AFTA was designed in large part to provide an ASEAN alternative, however modest, to the megamarkets being created in western Europe and North Amer-ica; its start-up, however, has disappointed some of its principal proponents. The initial idea was to reduce or eliminate tariffs on manufactured goods over fifteen years, meanwhile ignoring obsta-cles to trade in agricultural products and services, which were filled with political minefields of their own. Member states also retained unlimited rights to declare exceptions from the general agreement for specific manufactured items. By the time the starting date of January 1, 1993, had arrived, the exceptions were so numerous that even some of the initial proponents of AFTA were doubtful about the benefits that could be expected. The start was postponed by a year.

One lesson these initiatives might yield is that from a U.S. policy point of view, Southeast Asia must increasingly be viewed as an integral part of "greater East Asia." The United States stands to encounter many of the same opportunities, and many of the same difficulties, in dealing with Southeast Asia in the future that it has encountered in dealing with northeast Asia in the past, as the economies of the two regions become increasingly integrated be-cause of capital movements and changing patterns of business ownership. This has implications for how the United States carries on its economic diplomacy. Aside from its still active bilateral economic diplomacy, the principal forum for U.S. policy discussion clearly is the meetings of APEC. The United States can signal its recognition of the significance of this undertaking by sustaining the recent high level of its participation in APEC proceedings, and by actively participating in setting its agenda. A principal interest for the United States should be the development of a common understanding of what constitutes "fair investment." All the parties affected, including the United States, need to assess government subsidies that favor investment to produce exports for the U.S. market. APEC is well suited by its membership to address such topics.

But Southeast Asia cannot be subsumed altogether into "greater East Asia"; it also needs to be dealt with as an economic subregion apart from the whole. From the perspective of U.S. interests, Southeast Asia is qualitatively different from northeast Asia. It strongly welcomes American investors. U.S. exports to Southeast Asia are likely through the present decade to include major cases of government procurement. So at the same time that the United States moves to address issues that reach across "greater East Asia," it will also have an interest in issues that arise principally in Southeast Asia. The impact of NAFTA on the ASEAN economies is a case in point.

The principal lesson to be drawn from recent debate, in any case, is the need for positive thinking about U.S. trade policy. The U.S. economy is more than a market. And U.S. trade policy must amount to more than a set of rules about market access. The United States also is the world's largest producer of goods and services, and even in the present period of reduced savings is one of the world's largest sources of technology and investment capital. The global economy from which Americans have benefited so much depends on the continuity of American participation. And the U.S. economy can only stand to benefit from a general expansion of the flow of goods and services, and of capital and technology, to regions where the returns are highest, among which Southeast Asia is a world leader.

In short, if the Clinton administration and the Democratic leadership of the House and Senate are serious about promoting a resurgence of the American economy, nothing they could do would be more likely to achieve that purpose than to expand U.S. economic relations with Southeast Asia. Given the history of U.S. relations with the region, this will require political leadership. With the Seattle summit, the White House took a big step in helping to refocus U.S. attention on the Pacific economy. But much more is needed. Washington must take into account myriad other political, strategic, social, and cultural interests that also impinge on U.S. policy. It is to these that we now turn.

Chapter 6

Issues of Governance and the Protection of Human Rights

As important as economic priorities are in the new American agenda, no issues have had greater public visibility in the United States in recent years than those of human rights and democracy. The collapse of communism in eastern Europe and the dissolution of the Soviet Union led Americans and western Europeans to heightened expectations of rapid political as well as economic change elsewhere in the world. In this the West has been disappointed, and nowhere more seriously than in East and Southeast Asia: Leninist regimes persist in China, North Korea, and Vietnam, and authoritarian regimes remain in place in many other states of the region.

It followed that when Bill Clinton said he would give a higher priority to human rights than his recent predecessors, Southeast Asian governments began to take defensive action. Now, well into the Clinton presidency, it is appropriate to ask: What rights matter most, or should matter most, to the United States? And what can the United States do about them?

POLITICAL LEADERSHIP, STABILITY, AND CHANGE

The political history of Southeast Asia was interrupted by long periods of alien rule by colonial powers, and then by revolutionary

53

opposition to it, during the course of which the political institutions indigenous to the region's societies were largely destroyed. Of the many kingdoms, principalities, and sultanates, large and small, that flourished well into the nineteenth century, and often well into the twentieth, only the kingdom of Thailand, the recently restored monarchy of Cambodia, and the sultanates of Malaysia and Brunei survive. Family also survives as an occasional source of leadership succession, as in the case of Aung San Suu Kyi, the daughter of the founder of modern Burma. Otherwise Southeast Asia has lost its traditional political institutions and has yet to find stable modern replacements.

Another survivor of the turbulent past is the continuing role of the armed forces in the politics of most Southeast Asian countries. Thailand's army forced a constitution on that country's absolute monarch in the 1930s, provided the country with its prime ministers for decades thereafter, and remains a force to be reckoned with in the nation's politics. In Burma, Vietnam, and Indonesia, revolutionary armies fought for independence from the European powers in the late 1940s and early 1950s, later fought for national unity, and have played a role in national politics ever since. Only the Philippines, Malaysia, and Singapore became independent with a tradition of civilian control over professional military services; in the Philippines the long period of martial law in the 1970s seriously eroded that tradition.

The regime of Burma is the most praetorian. So thoroughly is the army in control that it could deflect student demonstrations by calling a national election in 1990, find to its surprise that a party challenging the army had won, and, not liking this outcome, simply cancel the result, in the meantime placing under prolonged house arrest a woman who led the opposition and is a winner of the Nobel Peace Prize. In Vietnam, army officers continue to hold many positions in the Communist Party leadership; even after the demobilization of up to half its personnel, the Vietnamese army is still much the largest in Southeast Asia. In Indonesia, President Soeharto, a retired general, and the Indonesian army are between them in full control of the country's political institutions, having led a violent attack on the political left after a failed coup in 1965, brought about the destruction of what was then the world's third-largest communist party, and remained as the dominant element in the government, the government's political party, and the electoral process.

In this environment, political parties of the kind familiar to Americans are notable for their absence in Southeast Asia. The most common political regime has been the single-party state. That was the pattern in recent decades in the Philippines and in Thailand; it is the pattern in Singapore and Indonesia today, and in Burma and Vietnam. In this system, parties are more or less synonymous with the government in power, and together they dominate a country's political life. Alternatives to the governing party either do not exist or are not permitted to have a real prospect of winning an election. The party and the upper bureaucracy are closely related through overlapping memberships. Political regimes of this description produced much of the explosive economic and social change in Southeast Asia in recent decades—and failed to do so, as well, in Vietnam, Burma, and Ferdinand Marcos's Philippines.

Some might say that the Philippines had, for some years after its independence, an American system of two national political parties and even rotating presidential power between them; but these "parties" were never more than extensions of the personalities of their leaders. They were not institutions of social weight; attachments to them were weak, and even presidential aspirants were known to jump from one to the other for short-term advantage. Then President Marcos, acting during martial law, replaced the two traditional political parties with a single government-supported party of his own. The cost seems to have been permanent. The reconstituted versions of the old parties have been among the major losers in the last two presidential elections in the Philippines in 1986 and 1992; the winners have been individuals who campaigned on personality grounds, in contests devoid of policy debate. Experience with political parties in Thailand has been markedly similar. Thai parties have demonstrated little in the way of either depth or permanence. They appear to be factions rather than parties, patron-client groups without ideological or programmatic consequence. Thus governments in both countries, which have been the most freely decided in Southeast Asia in recent years, have been coalitions of convenience rather than of purpose. How much focus either can sustain in its policy regime remains to be seen.

A variant from the single-party state or the weak multiparty system is Malaysia, where the Barisan Nasional (National Front) has been unbeatable since it was formed following racial riots in 1969. The Barisan is not a single party, but an enduring union in which the interests of parties representing the Malay, Chinese, and Indian populations are negotiated. The parties within it have been relatively democratic in their internal affairs, and parties outside it have had considerable freedom in challenging the government in elections. The case is of interest because it suggests one way in which multiethnic societies could evolve toward greater openness without reducing significantly the ability of government to ward off potential violence.

In these circumstances, much depends on the skill and wisdom of individual leaders. The recent history of the region has seen the rise of a generation of leaders skilled in economic management, of whom Soeharto of Indonesia, Lee Kuan Yew of Singapore, Mahathir Mohamad of Malaysia, and Prem Tinsulanon of Thailand have been prominent examples. Such men have reflected and even reinforced the political conservatism of their national elites. They have been traditional in their orientation; moderate and even cautious in their view of change; disposed toward maintaining existing styles, forms, and institutions; and inclined to place a high premium on orderly process and predictability.

This generation of leaders sought legitimacy by way of economic development, and they did so with a distinctive orientation. Government was assumed to have a large role in the management of the economy, but it was expected to be effective. The traditional bureaucracy was still a political force, but it was to serve the new economic program. State corporations were a national resource, but had to be made to serve the national economic interest. Political forces, including the armed forces, were to be mobilized on behalf of the national economic agenda. The private business sector, too, was incorporated in this vision of state and society united in a common economic cause.

Society has accepted such leadership because welfare has been greatly advanced in material terms; the leadership has been able to maintain its power with minimal use of force. At the same time, the general orientation of policy has been toward increasing the number of units in the economy and society capable of autonomous action within the confines of the political system—including an increase in the number, variety, and complexity of both government agencies and private groups—and increasing the differentiation among economic and social classes, functional specializations, and interest groups.

This "managed pluralism" of the past generation has resulted in phenomena noted earlier: very high rates of saving and investment, a widening openness to foreign investment and communication, a broadening of exports in terms of both products and markets, and rising per capita incomes; but also increasing longevity, rising levels of education, increasing urbanization, a growing middle class, and a growing privatization of the economic foundation of the national elites. Many of the rates of change involved have been among the highest in the world.

These characterizations are drawn principally from the ASEAN four—Indonesia, Malaysia, Singapore, and Thailand—and they are drawn broadly, as these countries differ among themselves in many economic, social, and political respects. But the broad process of change that has been occurring in these countries has been so striking, and the demonstration effect has been so powerful, that most leaders in the rest of the region have aspired to do the same, or have been obliged to give lip service to that goal.

Thus the policy foundations laid down in the Philippines in the last years of the presidency of Corazon Aquino, and the policy positions taken in the early days of the presidency of Fidel Ramos—basically involving the breakup of financial and industrial fiefdoms by ending their protection from foreign competition—are consciously modeled on the experience of the other ASEAN members. Vietnam under reformers such as Vo Van Kiet has been taking economic policy steps in the same direction. The new coalition leaders in Cambodia and even the military junta of Burma now subscribe to economic and social principles that are clearly intended to bring these countries, as well, the economic success of their neighbors.

Change on the scale experienced by the ASEAN four has major implications for their political systems and, if the other countries follow through on their currently indicated courses of action, for the entire region. The general direction is that of expanding the political elites, opening the contestation for public office, widening the process of consultation and consensus-building, and in other ways increasing the transparency of government. Recent economic and social change is contributing to pressures on political leaders to make adjustments in these directions. Elections are being contested more seriously. Private money is becoming more important to the contests. Candidates are being subjected to greater public scrutiny. Legislatures are demanding to be taken more seriously. Policies are increasingly likely to be questioned in the mass media. In varying degrees from country to country, a growing and widening demand is evident for greater openness in the political process.

The issue has been joined. The military and civilian bureaucracies are on the defensive in Southeast Asia, and the urban middle classes are on the rise. How long it will take for predominant power to move from the one to the other, and how smooth or turbulent the transition will be, is unknown, in part because the institutions to mediate the process are weak or nonexistent. Much continues to depend on the qualities of individual leaders, and as history reminds us, leadership is often found wanting.

This is not to say, however, that the change is necessarily distant for all. The political elites in Southeast Asia are not monolithic. An obvious pulling and tugging is going on between groups that would like to have more say about how their governments function, and groups that do not want to enlarge the access to power. Governing elites, by and large, hope they can have economic change, and perhaps some social change, without jostling the political arrangements that enable them to run things more or less as they have been doing. But most know they have to move in the direction of greater openness. Younger and better-educated citizens will demand greater respect for their rights, and abuses on the part of their governments will be seen as a sign of old political structures that they no longer identify with. A prominent example is Singapore, where 40 percent of the population voted against the government in elections since 1988.

THE UNITED STATES AND DEMOCRATIC GOVERNANCE

The principal U.S. policy in place derives from a provision in the annual foreign aid legislation that bans most forms of bilateral aid to a country when an elected government has been overthrown in a military coup. This provision was the basis for suspending economic assistance to Burma when its armed forces refused to permit the civilian government elected in May 1990 to take control. The same provision was used in suspending economic and military assistance to Thailand when a group of generals overthrew the elected government in February 1991. But U.S. aid is at such a low level in Southeast Asia that these actions had little or no effect. Arms and trade embargoes would have been more potent, but only as a collective measure, and none of the key regional governments were willing to go that far—not China, which was a major arms provider; nor Japan, which was a major source of aid and investment, although it did cut off new aid to Burma; nor the other Southeast Asian states, whose public silence lent more than a semblance of regional political support to the Burmese and Thai military leaders.

If Washington is to build an international coalition to support democratically elected civilian governments in this region, its work is cut out for it. But working on the problem, and seeking out positive measures that can be taken before force and violence intervene, is important. There is a connection between military rule and the violation of human rights. In Burma and Thailand, the overturning of election results by the armed forces was followed by major rights violations. The dominance of the Indonesian army in the governance of East Timor was a factor in the shootings of civilian demonstrators there. It is a responsibility of the U.S. armed forces to develop more explicit attention to the issues such cases raise for training programs in which Southeast Asian military personnel participate. In addition, it is regrettable that an ingredient missing from the democratic consensus on these recent occasions has been the government of Japan. The dominant Japanese view has been that it supports evolutionary political change through economic growth. But Tokyo also has been struggling to give more meaning to the principle of taking human rights into account in the administration of economic aid. The change in Japan's national politics in mid-1993 might provide an opening for movement here, and it is one the United States should actively seek.

One important area foreign aid donors should pay attention to is the development of institutions outside the state apparatus through which citizens can take action in their own interest. More aid agencies should be active in channeling funds in this direction: toward privately sponsored local organizations that carry on research and education on public policy issues; others that work with and give voice to nonelite groups in society; and programs of training and research that contribute to greater professionalism on the part of legislatures, judiciaries, and the mass media.

Possibly the most useful action the United States can take is to contribute to the freer distribution of information. State censorship and self-censorship are commonplace everywhere in Southeast Asia except Thailand and the Philippines. American-owned print media already represent a significant alternative source of international news for the English-speaking elite. When political crises occur, many members of this elite rely heavily on the Voice of America and the overseas service of the BBC for fast and reliable information. The extension of international television news to the region via satellite in the last few years represents a still further opening of the channels of communication, except in countries where it is inhibited or not legally permitted, which include Vietnam, Malaysia, and Singapore. The efforts of private book publishers in Southeast Asia to expand the range of serious political literature available to students and others also deserve continuing U.S. support.

A current issue for the United States is whether and how to expand U.S.-based radio reporting on the domestic affairs of East Asian nations. Government repression of the free exchange of information makes a prima facie case for others to provide expanded reportage on the domestic affairs many of these countries. But the proposal for a Radio Free Asia targeted on China, North Korea, and Vietnam would project the antagonisms of the Cold War into a new era. Independent television by satellite and videocasette is already eroding the power of governments to control the flow of information in the region. Given time it should be more effective than alternatives created by the U.S. government.

Notwithstanding such external pressures for change, the political fundamentals in Southeast Asia are not going to be altered by American diplomacy or the American media. For some time to come, citizens of much of the region are likely to face only limited degrees of freedom to organize political parties and to express their political opinions. The integrity of elections, the powers of legislatures, and the independence of the courts, like freedom of the press, are likely to be distant prospects. These are goals that the people of Southeast Asia are going to have to want for themselves, and want enough to struggle for themselves.

Americans also must remember that the United States has a role to play as exemplar that goes far beyond its ability to influence particular events. The American political system is on public display every day in the international marketplace of ideas. The performance of this political system, including its ability to meet the economic and social needs of the population, is closely watched in regions such as Southeast Asia. Leaders such as Foreign Minister Ali Alatas of Indonesia have taken the position that the human rights established by international covenant include not only civil and political rights, but also economic, social, and cultural ones; that these are of equal value and priority in the world at large; and that they must be applied in a manner that is broadly acceptable within the international community as a whole, meaning within both developing and developed societies.

Former Prime Minister Lee Kuan Yew of Singapore has gone further. In a speech in Manila at the end of 1992, he lectured his audience on the need for discipline rather than democracy in the interest of national development. "I believe that what a country needs to develop is discipline more than democracy," he said. "The exuberance of democracy leads to undisciplined and disorderly conditions which are inimical to development. The ultimate test of the value of a political system is whether it helps that society to establish conditions which improve the standard of living for the majority of its people, plus enabling the maximum of personal freedoms compatible with the freedoms of others in society."[59]

Such Southeast Asians are convinced that, when viewed in these terms, the performance of their governments has been of a high order. Some also suggest that the United States has not been doing nearly as well as they have in protecting economic and social rights, and insist that these be part of any discussion. The Los Angeles riots of 1992 had a serious impact on Southeast Asian thinking about the U.S. commitment to populist economic and social ideals. Americans need to remember that the case for democratic government, like that for a market economy, depends as much on what the United States does at home as on what it says abroad.

THE UNITED STATES AND HUMAN RIGHTS

Given the difference of philosophy between a Bill Clinton and a Lee Kuan Yew about what constitutes good government, the question remains as to what they might agree on in the area of human rights. Writing in mid-1993, Kishore Mahbubani, a senior official in the Singapore government, offered a personal answer to the question: "Both Asians and Westerners are human beings. They can agree on minimal standards of civilised behaviour that both would like to live under. For example, there should be no torture, no slavery, no arbitrary killings, no disappearances in the middle of the night, no shooting down of innocent demonstrators, no imprisonment without careful review. These rights should be upheld not only for moral reasons; there are sound functional reasons. Any society which is at odds with its people and shoots them down when they demonstrate peacefully, as Burma did, is headed for trouble."[60]

That expression of the views of an influential Singaporean made a promising start on a dialogue that is much needed. The governments of the United States and most Southeast Asian states remain far from agreeing on even this much about human rights, let alone on what should be done when they are infringed upon. In a lead-up to the June 1993 World Conference on Human Rights, which took place in Vienna, preparatory meetings were held in several regions of the world for the purpose of formulating "regional declarations." At the meeting of Asian nations in Bangkok, the consensus was that while unspecified human rights are universal, "they must be considered in the context of a dynamic and evolving process of international norm-setting, bearing in mind the significance of national and regional particularities and various historical, cultural and religious backgrounds."[61] The Bangkok Declaration also insisted on the principle of noninterference in the internal affairs of sovereign states, and rejected any linkage between human rights and foreign aid.

This approach was highly criticized in the United States and elsewhere, as well as by numerous nongovernmental organizations in Southeast Asia itself; the Vienna conference did, in the event, reaffirm the universality of rights as expressed in earlier UN declarations and conventions. But the Bangkok and Vienna meetings together highlighted the profound difference in views held by the United States and several Southeast Asia governments. U.S. Secretary of State Warren Christopher said in Vienna that there was a single standard of acceptable behavior all around the world, and that the United States would apply it to all countries. He went on to criticize unnamed challengers by saying, "We cannot let cultural relativism become the last refuge of repression."[62] Foreign Minister Ali Alatas of Indonesia rejected such criticism as "nebulous" and "spurious." The problem was, he suggested, that Western nations were applying a double standard, criticizing non-Western nations and meanwhile failing to do anything effective in Bosnia, where "an entire nation is being subjected to brutal aggression, mass murder, systematic rape and the inhuman practice of ethnic cleansing."[63]

In UN human rights negotiations, U.S. officials reportedly viewed not only China and Indonesia as adversaries, but also, to a lesser extent, Singapore, Malaysia, Burma, and Vietnam. Even the host of the Bangkok meeting, the elected prime minister of Thailand, supported the concept of an "Asian view" of human rights. Only the Philippines among Southeast Asian states supported the principle of universality. Japan, caught up in its desire to be a member both of the community of industrial democracies and of the Asia region, agreed to the Bangkok Declaration and also issued a statement to the effect that it did not support some positions in the document.

The problem was, of course, that most Southeast Asian governments are themselves guilty of some infringements of the rights of their own citizens. Considerations of realpolitik inhibit their neighbors from even acknowledging these infringements, let alone trying to do anything about them. The cases of Thailand, Burma, and Indonesia illustrate the dynamics at work.

Thailand

Thailand has not usually been considered among the countries of Southeast Asia with major human rights problems. In May 1992, however, army troops fired on crowds of unarmed civilians demanding the resignation of Suchinda Kraprayoon from the office of prime minister. Suchinda was commander of the army, supreme commander of the armed forces, and one of a group of generals who had overthrown the government of an elected prime minister in February 1991. He had recently arranged to have himself named prime minister. Action against the demonstrators quickly escalated from fire hoses to M-16 rifles. Over three days, army and border patrol police used high-performance weapons to clear the streets of the capital. Before the month was out, international pressure and the intervention of the king led to Suchinda's resignation. The death toll was still unknown a year later. A total of 52 bodies were recovered, but others were still unaccounted for—as many as 163, according to a group of families of the missing.[64]

The Bush administration condemned the violence and loss of life. Many Thai civilians in and out of government had hoped the United States would act even more forcefully and more publicly than it did. Apparently foreign intervention in internal affairs is not uniformly opposed; it seems to matter whose rights are being infringed upon. Also, no one in Bangkok seemed to be arguing in May 1992 that there was an "Asian view" of the military action against the civilian demonstrators. Even a senior officer in the armed forces command acknowledged that the Thai army had suffered a serious loss in public esteem as a result of the attack on the civilian demonstrators. It bears mentioning that a large number of personnel in the upper civil and military services of Thailand are American-educated and share many political values with Americans. These Thais were particularly critical of what they saw as a subdued U.S. response to the army coup and subsequent shootings. One civilian cabinet minister suggested that an earlier generation of American ambassadors would have been more forceful.[65]

Burma

By comparison with Thailand, Burma is a pariah state—in the words of an American rights organization, "one of the human rights disasters in Asia."[66] The Nobel Peace Prize winner Aung San Suu Kyi has been under house arrest since leading her party to victory in the national election of May 1990. Unknown numbers of political dissidents remain in prison. Former student protesters remain in privation on the border with Thailand. The Burmese military junta, known officially as the State Law and Order Restoration Council (SLORC), mounted offensives against major ethnic and religious minorities living in border areas. By June 1992, more than 300,000 refugees, most of them members of the Rohingya Muslim minority, were reportedly in search of refuge in neighboring Bangladesh. By September of that year, Burmese army operations against the Karen ethnic minority had created some 100,000 additional internal refugees in northeastern Burma and along the border with Thailand.

The Bush administration issued strong public condemnations of Burma's human rights practices, labeling the government one of the worst violators of human rights in the world. A 1992 State Department report on international narcotics control also named Burma as the largest source of opium and heroin in the world. In the UN Human Rights Commission and in the General Assembly, the United States voted for resolutions critical of Burmese human rights performance. U.S. Senate and House resolutions urged the president to seek an international arms embargo on Burma. Secretary of State Baker, meeting with the ASEAN foreign ministers in Manila in July 1992, appealed for a message to the Burmese military to release all political prisoners. Burma was kept from attending the meeting as an observer; otherwise the U.S. appeal went unheeded. The ASEAN ministers voted to continue their policy of "constructive engagement" with Burma.[67]

Indonesia

If Thailand represents a case of rights abuse in which the United States had considerable influence but was subdued in its reaction, and Burma a case in which the United States has acted vigorously but has only limited influence, Indonesia represents a more challenging sort. The United States has large and multiple interests in Indonesia, and has long enjoyed warm relations with its military-dominated government, which is responsible for continuing rights abuses on its geographic periphery.

International attention has focused on the eastern half of the small island of Timor in the lesser Sunda archipelago, which was abandoned by its longtime Portuguese colonizers and taken over by the Indonesians in 1975. East Timor is small in population and poor in resources. It was of little international interest in 1975, when the Portuguese left it in precipitate fashion and a local leftist movement, the Revolutionary Front for an Independent Timor (known by its Portuguese acronym, Fretilin), looked as though it would take over. The Indonesian army moved into East Timor at this point, with great force and extraordinary brutality; in the initial and ensuing violence, the death toll reached 100,000, which was one-sixth of the population, or about the share of the population that died in Cambodia under the rule of the Khmer Rouge.

The East Timor case might well have lingered more or less quietly on the international agenda for years. The Indonesians were investing heavily in education, hospitals, and roads in East Timor, funding the entire provincial budget from Jakarta, and beginning to create a modicum of development that was far in advance of anything that was seen while the Portuguese were in charge. This is how the situation might have stood for some time, that is, if it were not for the renewal of violence that occurred on November 12, 1991.

On that date, a funeral in Dili, the capital of East Timor, turned into a political demonstration against Indonesian control. Troops opened fire on the unarmed demonstrators, killing at least seventy-five. Two American journalists happened to be present, and they reported the incident to the world. Indonesian President Soeharto, who was traveling abroad at the time, was well aware of the international uproar created by the killings. On his return, he appointed a national commission of inquiry, which led to the dismissal of two senior army generals, and a council of military honor, which led to the courts-martial of ten army men involved in the shootings. These were important precedents, and initially it appeared that the dismissals and trials would be followed by others. In time, this proved not to be the case. Even worse, the judicial treatment of the army men (maximum sentence: eighteen months) proved to be out of all proportion to the treatment of young Timorese who organized a peaceful march in Jakarta to protest the killings (maximum sentences: nine to ten years).

These events were accompanied by a cascade of adverse U.S. reactions. In April 1992 Senator Claiborne Pell, chairman of the Foreign Relations Committee, and Senator David Boren, chairman of the Select Committee on Intelligence, were denied permission to visit East Timor, and in a call on Soeharto they told him that the situation was having a negative impact on U.S. relations. In June a bipartisan group of senators wrote Secretary of State Baker, urging that the United States make a strong public statement at a World Bank meeting of donor governments providing aid to Indonesia; at that meeting, in July, the U.S. delegation did so, alone among the donor delegations, although Canada boycotted the meeting altogether on the same grounds. In October, after a bitter disagreement that was settled only in conference committee, the Congress removed funds for U.S. military assistance to Indonesia from the foreign aid budget. The amount of money was only $2.3 million, but the action was more than symbolic. A senior Indonesian defense official remarked at the time that his country could easily pay for the training from its own funds but might not do so. And if training with U.S. forces did not continue, joint exercises with U.S. forces also were likely to go by the boards in a few years.[68]

In March 1993, in the Clinton administration's first act on a major human rights issue in Southeast Asia, the United States reversed a long-standing policy at the UN Human Rights Commission in Geneva. Having voted to block UN action on East Timor as recently as the previous year, the United States on this occasion voted for the first time in favor of a resolution that expressed "deep concern" about human rights violations in East Timor.[69] The resolution, which carried by twenty-two votes to twelve, with fifteen abstentions, also expressed regret at the disparity in the severity of sentences given to civilians and military personnel, and called for greater access to the territory for UN and other observers. Canada and Australia also voted for the resolution; Japan abstained. The impact was not immediately apparent. A month later, the *New York*

Times printed a dispatch from Dili on its front page under the headline, "Fear and Repression Still Rule Area Occupied by Indonesia."[70]

East Timor will remain a live issue in the United States. That was assured by the change in administration, as well as by change in the Congress. Bill Clinton and Al Gore both expressed themselves before their election as critical of Indonesia's performance in East Timor. The new chairman of the House Subcommittee on East Asia and the Pacific, Gary Ackerman, did the same. For a time it seemed possible that the independence movement in Timor was losing steam. In June 1993 Indonesian authorities captured and sentenced to life imprisonment the leader of the Fretilin guerrilla army, Jose Alexandre Gusmão. Nevertheless, Amnesty International reported that systematic oppression was continuing. In July, meeting in Tokyo with President Soeharto, President Clinton raised concerns about conditions in East Timor. Later in the month, the State Department confirmed that it had blocked the sale of four used F-5 planes to Indonesia. The action was taken for multiple reasons, including Indonesian attempts to sell arms to Iran, but human rights concerns also were mentioned. The point was not lost on Jakarta. On August 13 President Soeharto reduced the Gusmão sentence to twenty years.

It is within the capacity of the two governments to address the larger question of the direction of U.S.-Indonesian relations before more such events take their toll. During the fall of 1993 a move was under way in the U.S. Senate that would make U.S. arms sales of all kinds to Indonesia conditional on progress in dealing with U.S. human rights concerns. Senators Charles Robb and Richard Lugar argued that military assistance to Indonesia ought to be viewed in terms of a wide range of factors. The Indonesian government announced that if the proposed legislation became law, Indonesia would have no choice but to buy arms from other nations. It was clearly time for the leaders of the two nations to take preventive action. The United States was in need of an official policy approach that had the sweep of the Robb-Lugar statement. Indonesia was in need of a policy that could attract more confidence in UN-sponsored talks on Timor. Failure could lead to a continued downward spiral in relations from which neither party, or the cause of human rights, would benefit.

AN ABSENCE OF CONSENSUS

Human rights abuses in Thailand, Burma, and Indonesia demonstrate the extreme diversity of conditions and circumstances in the region, and of American strengths and weaknesses. The United States had considerable leverage in Thailand after the army coup of February 1991, and especially after the army fired on civilian demonstrators in May 1992. Washington probably did not exercise its influence as quickly or as forcefully as it might have done. But the case is not generalizable. It is difficult to imagine Washington's having such influence in any other country of Southeast Asia in similar circumstances, with the possible exception of the Philippines.

In Burma, on the other hand, the United States has no leverage on the human rights situation and must try to build a coalition of political and economic opposition. A coalition led by the ASEAN states was eventually effective in causing Vietnam to withdraw its troops from Cambodia in 1989, but there is no prospect of an ASEAN coalition against the Burmese military. The Cold War is over, and regional states such as Indonesia and Malaysia are no longer of a mind to see eye to eye politically with the United States. Indonesia in particular faces the added difficulty that faulting Burma on human rights would seem to some rather like the pot calling the kettle black. Any coalition would have to include Japan in order to embargo aid, and would have to include China in order to embargo arms, and neither of these is feasible. Even if the United States could convince Japan and China, the absence of Burma's ASEAN neighbors would make any embargo ineffective.

The case of East Timor is much more complex than either of these, in that the United States and Indonesia share multiple interests but have only very limited influence over each other. Washington did undoubtedly play a role in denying President Soeharto a place on the schedule of the July 1993 Group of 7 heads of government meeting in Tokyo—a place the Indonesians had sought assiduously for Soeharto as the current leader of the Non-Aligned Movement. Such prices could no doubt continue to be exacted on both sides, and a spiral of criticism and countercriticism would follow, from which neither side would benefit. To avoid that, the United States must make it clear to the government of Indonesia that it will maintain a close watch on the situation in East Timor, and it must give substance to that intention by demanding frequent opportunities for U.S. government personnel to visit East Timor and by supporting international measures of inspection and assessment, particularly any measures that the UN Human Rights Commission may undertake. Washington also must make it unmistakably clear to the government of Indonesia that it will consider Jakarta responsible for any repetition of the abuse of unarmed civilians by military personnel anywhere in Indonesia and that it will link its future decisions on economic and security relations to progress regarding human rights. Any lobbyist in Washington worth his or her salt would be telling the Indonesians the same thing.

Given the difficulty in formulating a regional strategy with such a variety of situations, the United States should use the lack of a conceptual and political consensus in the region to its advantage. Nonofficial dialogue could be an effective form of regional action. Dialogue among policy analysts who are politically close to their governments but do not represent them officially is a well-traveled route among the United States, Japan, and the ASEAN states. Dialogue at the level of the Asia-Pacific region would involve industrial democracies such as the United States, Japan, and Australia, as well as developing countries that exhibit varying degrees of authoritarianism, such as the ASEAN states. Eventually such Leninist regimes as those of China and Vietnam would need to be included. This is not a means to resolving the problem of protecting human rights in Southeast Asia. It is only a way of starting to sort out the issues. But it is a way to start.

The United States faces a major challenge in its efforts to protect human rights in Southeast Asia. The task would be much easier if civil government were everywhere in control of the region's armed forces. That is still a distant prospect. Washington can take certain steps that will speed democraticization, especially in ensuring the free flow of information. But so long as armed force is not controlled by effective political institutions, flagrant abuse is bound to occur from time to time. The international community is very far from a consensus about what to do when that occurs in Southeast Asia. Concerned Americans and Southeast Asians face a long process of dialogue and mutual education.

Chapter 7

The New Strategic Balance

The end of the Cold War has brought to Southeast Asia a whole series of departures in thought and action regarding national and international security. Domestic threats to the established governments of the region have receded in significance as the world has grown weary of armed insurgencies. Local threats to the peaceful order of the region have evaporated with the Vietnamese withdrawal from Cambodia. External threats have declined with the Russian departure from air and naval bases in Vietnam. As much as any region in the world, Southeast Asia today finds itself in a condition of unfamiliar peace. Southeast Asia is without the presence of a major foreign military installation for the first time since the Portuguese took Malacca in present-day Malaysia in 1511.

Domestic security threats do continue to preoccupy the military leaders of some countries. The military government of Burma faces continuing ethnic separatist movements along its borders. The new coalition government of Cambodia faces a continuing threat of uncertain proportions from the once dominant Khmer Rouge. In the Philippines, a minority faction of the once powerful Communist Party continues to espouse armed insurrection, although its capability is now reduced to rural banditry. And in Indonesia, the central government is confronted on its remote peripheries by separatist movements in Aceh and Irian and by a continuing resistance to its annexation of East Timor. But given the regional and extraregional environment, these domestic threats are less potent as destabilizing tendencies today than they have been at any time in recent decades.

Similarly, the prospect of regional sources of threats to international security is much reduced. The withdrawal of Vietnam from Cambodia was a direct result of the end of the Cold War, and especially of a decision by Russia and China to seek improved relations with the West. Other regional sources of potential instability are limited for much the same reasons. The economic benefits of amity are considerable among the ASEAN members, too considerable for any of these states to permit their problems with each other to get out of hand. Burma and Vietnam are seeking to improve their relations with these same neighboring states in large part out of a desire to share in the economic benefits these states have enjoyed. This is not to say there are no problems with border populations or no cases of conflicting territorial claims, but they are minor for the most part, and politically contained.

In these circumstances, a growing number of Southeast Asian leaders and analysts are focusing on the future capabilities and intentions of China, Japan, and even India. ASEAN leaders have made a considerable effort to balance the American departure from the Philippines with U.S. access to alternate air and naval facilities in other ASEAN countries. A significant shift has begun in investment, and in talk of investment, to enhance ASEAN air and naval capabilities. The leaders of the ASEAN states have for the first time put regional security on their own joint agenda, and obtained agreement to a dialogue on the subject with the major external powers. These developments together constitute a major shift in the regional security equation, in which the ASEAN states themselves are acquiring the principal responsibility for the security of the region, and with it a stronger voice in shaping the new strategic balance in East Asia and the Pacific.

The United States has for the past half century had two security interests in Southeast Asia. One has been that no other power or combination of powers should dominate East Asia, including Southeast Asia, and the western Pacific. The other has been that the U.S. navy and air force should enjoy freedom of transit through

Southeast Asia. The United States shares with the ASEAN states some of their current concerns about the potential rise of other powers external to the region. Washington appreciates the facilitation of transit through the air and waters of Southeast Asia that has been made possible by agreements reached with Singapore, Malaysia, and Indonesia, and particularly those of long standing with Thailand, which were of genuine significance as recently as the Gulf War. At the same time, especially in view of U.S. behavior with respect to Bosnia, Somalia, and Haiti, no one any longer imagines that the armed forces of the United States are likely to be employed in any military action in mainland or insular Southeast Asia in the foreseeable future. Only a vestige of ambiguity hangs over the case of possible Chinese aggression in the South China Sea.

Given its inhibitions, the United States has a responsibility to contribute as best it can to regional security in Southeast Asia. Possible lines of action obviously include the continuation of U.S. military training programs, U.S. military equipment sales, joint U.S.–Southeast Asian military exercises, and other confidence-building measures, including U.S. promotion of the transparency of Asian military budgets and arms transfers. But all this will occur to some extent without any change in U.S. policy. What is needed in addition, in the new environment, is continued reaffirmation of U.S. readiness to sustain its present security posture in the Pacific, and evidence of renewed U.S. political and economic commitment to the Pacific Community.

CHANGING FORCE STRUCTURES

Having been developed largely in response to domestic and regional threats to security, the armed forces of Southeast Asia have been composed predominantly of land forces. Yet all these force structures are undergoing change today. Vietnam has had a particularly large army by world standards. As recently as 1988, the army of Vietnam was reported to number 1.2 million, making it the third-largest in the world (after those of China and the Soviet Union). Following its partial demobilization, the Vietnamese army has been said to number 600,000, still a very large number by Southeast

Asian standards. Thailand has had a relatively large number of men under arms by regional standards ever since the Vietnamese invaded Cambodia (see Table 10); the Thai army is reportedly planning a long-term reduction of 25 percent. Indonesia, in spite of its large population and great geographical size and its several separatist movements, but reflecting its distance from its neighbors, has had only a slightly larger number under arms. And the Philippines, which has faced the largest insurgency in the region, but also is distant from neighbors, has had still fewer under arms. This is the strongest evidence that domestic threats have been of limited con-

TABLE 10—ARMED FORCES AND POPULATION, 1979 AND 1989

Country and year	Armed forces (thousands)	Population (millions)	Armed forces per 1,000 population
Indonesia			
1979	250	151.4	1.7
1989	285	186.7	1.5
Malaysia			
1979	82	13.4	6.1
1989	110	17.1	6.4
Philippines			
1979	156	49.5	3.2
1989	106	63.0	1.7
Singapore			
1979	57	2.4	23.9
1989	56	2.7	20.7
Thailand			
1979	250	46.0	5.4
1989	273	55.2	4.9
World			
1979	26,700	4,380	6.1
1989	28,300	5,200	5.4
Developing countries			
1979	16,700	3,300	5.1
1989	18,300	4,040	4.5

Source: U.S. Arms Control and Disarmament Agency, *World Military Expenditures and Arms Transfers 1990* (Washington, D.C., 1991), Tables 1 and 3.

cern. Only Malaysia and Singapore, reflecting their small populations, were above world averages in the ratio of armed forces to
population.

The military expenditures of most Southeast Asian states,
given the American security umbrella, also have been modest by
world standards (see Table 11). The spending of Indonesia, the
Philippines, and Malaysia has been particularly modest—on the
order of less than 3 percent of GNP and about 10 percent of central
government expenditures in recent years. Thailand's military budget has been higher only as a proportion of central government

TABLE 11—MILITARY EXPENDITURES (ME), 1979 AND 1989

Country and year	ME (millions of dollars)	ME as % of GNP	ME as % of central government expenditures
Indonesia			
1979	957	3.3	13.7
1989	1,510	1.7	8.2
Malaysia			
1979	490	3.8	14.4
1989	1,039	2.9	10.0
Philippines			
1979	518	2.3	16.8
1989	960	2.2	12.1
Singapore			
1979	427	4.9	21.1
1989	1,475	5.1	18.9
Thailand			
1979	854	4.2	23.6
1989	1,843	2.7	17.7
World			
1979	528,700	5.2	19.2
1989	1,035,700	4.9	17.4
Developing countries			
1979	99,500	5.7	20.1
1989	167,700	4.3	14.5

Source: U.S. Arms Control and Disarmament Agency, World Military Expenditures and
Arms Transfers 1990 (Washington, D.C., 1991), Table 1.

expenditure, reflecting the relatively small share of GNP consumed by the government of Thailand.

Singapore's military spending has been spectacular in absolute and relative terms, enabling it to develop what are far and away the strongest air and naval forces in the region. At close to $1.5 billion or more a year, Singapore's military budget is almost as large as that of Indonesia or Thailand, each of which has a vastly larger population, a vastly larger area to defend, and a larger standing army. As a result, none of Singapore's neighbors has an air force or navy that is at all capable of challenging it in conventional terms. By 1995, Singapore will have more than 200 military aircraft, most of which probably will be devoted to medium-range maritime operations. It has for some years been the only country in the region capable of wide-ranging aerial search and surveillance. In addition, Singapore has armed some of its aircraft with antiship missiles and fitted them for midair refueling. Singapore currently has a unique capacity for operations well into the South China Sea.[71] The principal security threat to Singapore is a recrudescence of ethnic violence in neighboring Malaysia, which could spill over into Singapore and could draw Indonesia into its wake. That would be likely only if Malaysia's economy were to become unraveled, which is far from the current prospect. Singapore therefore seems to some, recalling the country's ties to Israel, to be following a strategic policy of arming itself to the teeth.

According to a senior defense official, Singapore's military budget has a life of its own: "We are small compared with our neighbors. It's important for our psychic solace that we have an air umbrella and free sea lanes. . . . The question is when is enough enough? We spend six percent of GDP, a share that was settled in the late sixties. If the economy grows, we get an increase, Cold War or no. It's independent of perceived threats."[72]

Malaysia's leadership has watched Singapore's buildup with growing envy and suspicion. The Malaysian government has for years kept its military spending under firm budgetary control; even after writing a dramatic agreement with Britain in 1989 to buy $4.4 billion in military hardware, Malaysian leaders moved cautiously from year to year, with cost considerations evidently much in mind. However, Malaysia is expected to acquire upgraded versions of fighter/ground-attack aircraft in 1994 and what would be the most sophisticated frigates in the region in 1996. Moreover, major purchases of high-performance U.S. and Russian fighter aircraft are in the offing. Announcements in mid-1993 put Malaysia's planned defense budget as rising to 4 percent of GDP in 1994 and to 6 percent thereafter.[73]

As this indicates, attitudes in Kuala Lumpur are changing, and multiple reasons are mentioned for this change. The Malaysian economy has been doing very well, and with the second-highest level of per capita income in Southeast Asia, the government can afford to pay for an upgrading of its forces out of increased income. The need to modernize various sorts of aircraft has built up over time. The political falling out between Kuala Lumpur and the political leaders of the oil-rich state of Sabah has reactivated long-term security concerns about East Malaysia. Recent Chinese policy toward the South China Sea has led Malaysians to question whether they could defend their claims there. Finally, the Russians have been offering fighter planes, helicopters, and other aircraft at bargain prices.[74] At this writing, Malaysia reportedly has decided to purchase eighteen MiG29s from the Russians and eight F-18s from McDonnell Douglas. Malaysia's defense minister has said his nation intends to make its air force a credible air power by the year 2000.

An air and naval buildup also is beginning in Thailand. The buildup is highlighted by Thailand's purchase of a helicopter carrier from Spain, and Sikorsky Seahawk helicopters from the United States to go with it. A second carrier also is planned. But more is involved. The Thai navy has acquired frigates from China and missiles from France. The Thai air force has a second squadron of F-16 fighters on order and plans an air base in the south to accommodate them. Most recently it placed an order for three U.S. early warning and control aircraft, at a cost of $680 million, becoming the second ASEAN country after Singapore to do so. Coupled with the planned reduction in Thailand's land forces, these acquisitions reflect a rising concern to improve the monitoring and defense of economic zones in the Gulf of Thailand and the western approaches in the Andaman Sea. More generally, the Thai plans also reflect

China's stated intention of building a blue-water navy and expectations of a reduced presence in the region of the U.S. Seventh Fleet.[75]

Indonesia's military leaders still see the principal threats to the security of the country as domestic in location and as political, economic, and social in nature. "People need to see security as a whole," a senior defense official said. "The army is the last resort. . . . Our philosophy since 1965 has been to give priority to political stability, economic development, and social equity. Stability has been our number-one aim until now. But it is no longer our principal concern. Economic development is number one. And right behind that is better distribution of income."[76]

But Indonesia's investments in air and naval power are changing. Indonesia has been producing maritime patrol aircraft under license from Spain; acquiring submarines from Germany and frigates from the Netherlands; and purchasing missiles for various missions from the United Kingdom, France, and the United States.[77] Indonesia's ambitious minister for research and technology, Bachruddin Habibie, has bought thirty-nine warships from the former East Germany (its entire surface fleet) and announced plans to spend $1.1 billion on a major program to overhaul them. Given Habibie's well-known commitment to high technology, his continued rise in power would greatly strengthen the prospects for further air and naval expansion in Indonesia, argued on the same grounds as in Thailand.[78]

The rest of Southeast Asia has no prospects of air or naval modernization. The principal security concern of the Philippines has been its domestic insurgency, and its external preoccupation has until recently been with the future of the U.S. bases on its territory; meanwhile, the country's economy has severely restricted Manila's ability to alter its military spending. As a senior member of the Philippine senate said, "We are strategically naked."[79] In the words of a senior defense official, "We do not even have the means to deal with piracy and smuggling."[80] Similarly, Vietnam and Burma are unlikely candidates for air and naval modernization at any time soon, although Hanoi's long-term ambitions are a matter of concern to its neighbors.

Thus the prevailing situation in the region is one of no near-term threat or perceived threat to the security of any country, but rather the absence of threats; yet an air and naval buildup has taken place in Singapore, is beginning to take place in Malaysia and Thailand, and may be in prospect in Indonesia. Some increase in air and naval capabilities in the region is desirable, so long as it is openly acknowledged and mutually acceptable. For example, joint patrols by the Indonesians and Singaporeans are said to have brought a dramatic reduction in piracy in the heavily used waters near Singapore. In the same way, these countries and Malaysia have a direct interest in the security of the Strait of Malacca, including its protection from oil pollution. As new economic development schemes are implemented, linking North Sumatra and peninsular Malaysia with southern Thailand, and eastern Malaysia and Indonesia with the southern Philippines, the need for policing the region's waterways might be expanded substantially.

At the same time, many of the recent equipment purchases made and orders placed are unrelated to such missions. Many of the planes and ships being added to the fleets of the wealthier ASEAN states are intended primarily for use up to a decade or more into the future, against any of several possible adversaries at a distance. They are primarily a response to the changing strategic balance in the region, and spending on them will be curtailed only as confidence in the stability of the regional order, which has been shaken by the end of the Cold War, is restored.

ASEAN'S SECURITY ROLE

It is important to take note of one additional local factor in the security situation of Southeast Asia: the multifaceted success of the ASEAN countries. If security is viewed as a whole, to use the Indonesian defense official's phrase, the security of Southeast Asia has been improved because of political and economic developments; those of recent decades have given great self-confidence to the ASEAN states, particularly to Singapore, Malaysia, Thailand, and Indonesia. Second only to the successes of domestic policy from country to country has been that of ASEAN itself. The integrity of borders has been assured, neighboring leaders have developed personal relationships, and large parts of the bureaucracies of the member states have participated in building a regional consensus of shared values, known as "the ASEAN spirit." Included in this process have been the military bureaucracies. Throughout the Cold War, ASEAN was carefully protected as an organization from any activities that would cause it to be seen as a military pact. On a bilateral basis, however, substantial relations have developed among the members' military establishments. According to knowledgeable sources in the region, these have included exchanges between training institutions, sharing of intelligence, and numerous joint training exercises. With the Cold War a thing of the past, the heads of the ASEAN governments have agreed to include senior officers of their military establishments in periodic meetings as a further confidence-building measure. A wide range of other measures also is under consideration to promote security cooperation among ASEAN members, short of a mutual security agreement. Included are the creation of a subunit of the ASEAN senior officials' meetings that would deal exclusively with security matters; intensive sharing of nonsensitive information, including major procurement decisions; notification of and attendance at neighboring and bilateral military exercises; and joint efforts in the supply and maintenance of defense hardware, including the production of spare parts and components. Taken together, these steps would create a major alteration of ASEAN, raising the stakes of its success or failure, and binding the future of its members to a degree unknown in the past.

The self-confidence of the ASEAN states, and their concern for the strategic balance in the wider region of East Asia and the Pacific, were both made further evident in July 1993, when the foreign ministers of the six nations voted to found the ASEAN Regional Forum. The new organization would aim in its membership and agenda to encompass the security of the whole of the Asia-Pacific region. Much was purposely left vague for the start, but the act was already a giant step in the direction of the first official, regionwide talks about defense arrangements and conflict management in the Pacific.

Washington has every reason to be supportive of these ASEAN initiatives. As Secretary of State Christopher said in Singapore in July 1993, all the nations of the Pacific now have an opportunity to "create a new regional balance that promotes stability, regional arms control and the peaceful resolution of disputes."[81] In Southeast Asia, that goal will be advanced by steadfast U.S. security relations with the ASEAN states, the integration with them of the Indochina states, and an increase in U.S. economic and political investment in both.

THE U.S. STRATEGIC INTEREST

The U.S. strategic interest in the western Pacific has historically been focused on northeast Asia, on China and Japan. During the nineteenth century most of Southeast Asia was colonized by European powers, and it was to these that the United States had to look for market access and protection of the sea lines of communication. The American colonization of the Philippines at the turn of the century did little to alter this perspective; one of the principal arguments for U.S. acquisition of the Philippine islands was that they would serve as stepping-stones to China. The prosecution of the Second World War in the Pacific reflected the same priorities; except for the Philippines, to which General Douglas MacArthur had pledged he would return, American forces bypassed Southeast Asia in favor of efforts to support the Kuomintang in China and to position themselves for a final assault on the home islands of Japan. The subsequent tragic involvement in Vietnam was predictably pursued in the name of a larger purpose: the containment of an expansive communist power backed by the Soviet Union and China.

Historically, then, U.S. policy has tended very strongly to view Southeast Asia in the wider context of East Asia and the Pacific, in which China and Japan have bulked large in demographic, economic, and military terms. And the underlying principle of U.S. policy has been that this wider region should not be dominated by any single foreign power or combination of foreign powers.

Contemporary American analysis does not challenge these priorities. Japan is the largest economy in the world after that of the United States, and the principal security partner of the United States in Asia—some would say its most important bilateral partner. China is the last remaining potential superpower in the world in terms of its population size, potential economic product, and possession of nuclear weapons. These are potent claims upon American attention. The principal questions Americans face as they look west-

ward across the Pacific have to do with how the United States should
position itself vis-à-vis these two Asian giants.[82] And it is primarily
in this context that U.S. strategic analysts view Southeast Asia.[83]

The one exception is traditionally expressed in terms of the sea
lanes between the Pacific and Indian Oceans. These are principally
the Strait of Malacca, which serves the bulk of surface traffic
through the region, and the lesser-known Lombok and Ombai-
Wetar Straits through the Indonesian archipelago, which serve
some surface traffic and are deep enough for nuclear submarines.
But the main threat to the Strait of Malacca is the heavy volume of
traffic that is using it, which is already resulting in increasing
numbers of collisions and oil spills, and the bordering states share
with the strait's users an interest regarding traffic there. A political-
military threat to any of these straits is likely to arise only in the
event of some wider breakdown in order in the region. Similarly,
with the increasing U.S. focus on rapid deployment, air transit
through Southeast Asia will be a growing U.S. interest, as it was
during the Gulf War. And access to military airfields during major
security crises is particularly dependent on political stability. So the
United States has a strategic interest in the stability of Southeast
Asia, focused on the nations bordering the principal straits and on
those providing access for air transit. This includes an interest in the
ability of ASEAN to sustain the stability of the region.

Only a threat to the independence and stability of the Southeast Asian region as a whole would threaten these U.S. strategic
interests. The United States is not going to become seriously involved in disputes between Southeast Asian states; it is difficult to
imagine the occurrence there of anything like the Gulf War. The
only reason for the United States to maintain a forward presence in
the western Pacific is to avoid a major shift in the balance of power in
the region, and the only states that could cause such a shift are
China and Japan. Both nations are stepping up their efforts to be of
influence in Southeast Asia, and governments there have already
begun to see both as having increased strategic interest of their
own.[84]

The main question is how the United States will respond to an
increased Chinese or Japanese presence. In the words of one analyst
from the region: "There is enormous goodwill toward the United

States in Southeast Asia. But the hard feeling is that China and Japan are here to stay, and these two countries will have to be dealt with. One is not clear whether the United States is in fact a reliable player in this equation. . . . It's not so much the size of the presence that the United States has in Southeast Asia, it's the perception. And the perception right now is of the United States in withdrawal.[85]

Specialists tend to see China as preoccupied with political and economic problems at home, needing improved relations with its Asian neighbors, wanting to be accepted in regional bodies, hoping to strengthen economic ties, and unlikely to pursue expansionist aims. From this perspective, current Chinese relations with the whole of Southeast Asia are the best they have been since 1949.[86] On the other hand, China's domestic stability remains uncertain as it makes its way through a generational change in the leadership of its government and ruling party. And in the new era of geoeconomics, China does not loom as a necessarily positive force from a Southeast Asian point of view. Its wage levels put it in a position to outcompete much of Southeast Asia with low-cost products in the U.S. market. It is not much of a market for Southeast Asian products. Also, China is beginning to attract significant investment capital in competition with Southeast Asia.

In addition, the states of Southeast Asia are not homogeneous in terms of their proximity to China or the degree to which their societies have been able to assimilate their resident Chinese. Three large states of mainland Southeast Asia—Burma, Thailand, and Vietnam—have moved somewhat closer to Beijing since the demise of the Soviet Union, reflecting China's enhanced weight in the wake of that event. Each, however, also has reasons to wish to limit the political influence of so near and powerful a neighbor; the Vietnamese are particularly sensitive to Chinese influence, not only because of centuries of Chinese colonization, but also because of the Chinese effort as recently as 1979 to "teach Vietnam a lesson" by sending troops across the border. Meanwhile the insular states, particularly Malaysia and Indonesia, have been consistent in maintaining their distance from China. Malaysia's domestic race relations continue to be narrowly balanced between the Malay majority and the large Chinese minority, and Indonesia's race relations remain potentially volatile because its resident Chinese, although only a small minority, are an unusually wealthy one.

While the Southeast Asian states are thus divided geopolitically and racially in their views of China and the Chinese, they may be united in their fear of China as a growing regional power. The Chinese are acquiring an enhanced capacity for conventional force projection, made possible by their rapid economic growth and by the availability of advanced weapons systems from Russia at affordable prices. Chinese passage of a territorial law in February 1992, reaffirming China's claim to the Spratly archipelago in the South China Sea, revived apprehensions about Beijing's long-term intentions. The attraction is the hope of finding oil or natural gas, as well as expanding national economic zones under the Law of the Sea; Brunei, Malaysia, the Philippines, Taiwan, and Vietnam also claim parts of the archipelago. Even nonclaimants have reason for concern; as a defense official in one such Southeast Asian country put it, the dispute could become a shooting conflict, sea lanes would be disturbed, Japanese shipping would be diverted, the price of oil would go up, and economic plans would be set awry. The ASEAN foreign ministers, meeting in July 1992, suggested that discussion of sovereignty be postponed while arrangements are worked out for cooperation in exploration and resource development. The Chinese have taken this same position. Meanwhile, in May 1993, a first scientific meeting was held on marine research as part of an effort to keep the political dimensions of the dispute under control.[87]

The Southeast Asians would not be able to deal to their satisfaction with an aggressive China at any time soon. Growth in the potency and reach of their weaponry over the next decade might permit them to prohibit the Chinese from the southern tier of the Spratlys, but China has a larger economy than Southeast Asia and a proportionately greater capacity to build its armed forces. The Southeast Asians would have greater influence diplomatically to the extent they could act from a position of agreement among themselves, as they did in opposing Vietnam's occupation of Cambodia, but the geopolitics of the region might make a common front against China difficult to achieve. For Southeast Asia, therefore, the best strategy is to engage China as a participant in regional affairs, and increase the incentives for it to find continuing economic and political benefits in its present, peaceful course. That is what the ASEAN states are doing in joining other nations of the region in APEC and, particularly, in sponsoring the ASEAN Regional Forum. Engaging China on a wide economic and political front also is one of the aims of the U.S. government. So the ASEAN states and Washington are pursuing mutually supportive strategies in dealing with China, and that is likely to enhance the prospects for their success.

THE BURDEN ON JAPAN

Unless the United States reverses the perception that it is withdrawing as a military presence in the region, however, a growing burden in balancing China will fall on Japan. And Japan has interests in Southeast Asia that are crucial to its security. Two-thirds of its crude oil and more than half of its iron ore pass through the straits of the region. Japan depends on Southeast Asia as a source of other important raw materials, as the locus of substantial investments, and as its third-largest trading partner (after the United States and the European Community). Peace and stability in Southeast Asia are thus important to Japan, and in maritime Southeast Asia they are essential.[88] At the same time, Japan labors under disabilities in Southeast Asia. Its economic predominance is a source of some unease in the region, even as its aid, trade, and investment are appreciated as a source of prosperity. Japan's concern for the security of its sea lanes has so far not been convertible into naval deployments into the Southeast Asian archipelago, even though its military budget is one of the largest in the world.

Japan also must take account of China. Given that China already has the second-largest economy in Asia, a large submarine fleet, a nuclear weapons capability, and the only permanent seat of an Asian power on the UN Security Council, China cannot be ignored by Japan. And China has been consistently suspicious of Japan's intentions and potential capability.

The principal obstacle to an expanded role for the armed forces of Japan lies within Japan itself. Many in Southeast Asia viewed the prospect of a Japanese role with the UN peacekeeping forces in Cambodia as acceptable. Some also have privately expressed the view that a Japanese naval and air presence in the region is inevitable over time.[89] But the consensus view is that the U.S.-Japan security treaty is of paramount importance to Southeast Asia. If that should break down, Southeast Asians would have to deal with a very different Japan. Thus ASEAN views on relations with Japan are conditioned heavily on keeping the United States in the region.[90]

"The United States should not 'leave' Southeast Asia just like that," one ASEAN defense minister has said. "Small disagreements could become big ones. A regional power could take over the role of the Americans. For example, Japan could change the balance if it were pushed. The Chinese might try them out—in the Paracels or Spratlys. We have to count on the Americans to discourage this sort of thing. U.S.-Japan relations should stay as they are—to keep Japan from 'going haywire.' But the United States won't be here indefinitely. We hope to have ten or fifteen years to build up our capacity and confidence. The next generation of leaders in this region will see that as its priority."[91]

"We have been a beneficiary of Japanese strength," according to another ASEAN defense minister. "Of course, there are three Japans—past, present, and future. Our people suffered in World War II, and they still remember. Japan's reluctance to come to terms with its past is a serious concern for us. Their people don't know about the brutality of the occupation. And what are we to expect of a Japan that knows nothing of its own past? The psyche of a nation docs not change in a generation. So, will Japan rearm? I am not sanguine. The U.S. relationship can't stay as it is. So how the Japanese arm is important. It would be okay if links with the United States continue strong. Right now we are at a level I would describe as 'concerned.' They could do it again. Whether in business or war, they are a dedicated people."[92]

In spite of these reservations, Southeast Asian relations with Japan are at a historic high. Japanese aid, trade, and investment have helped Indonesia, Malaysia, and Thailand in particular to achieve their high rates of economic growth. ASEAN acceptance also has been important to Japan's peacekeeping role in Cambodia. As a result, Japan has been able to take a number of initiatives with the confidence it would have ASEAN support: encouraging help to the economies of Vietnam, Cambodia, and Laos; expressing concern over China's military buildup and its involvement in the Spratly dispute; reaffirming its intention to maintain the Japan-U.S. security relationship; and, at the same time, announcing that it will take part actively in dialogue among the countries of the Asia-Pacific region regarding the region's peace and security.

THE U.S. SECURITY PRESENCE

There are thus two underlying and conflicting views in the ASEAN capitals regarding the United States vis-à-vis the end of the Cold War. One is that a "power vacuum" threatens to arise in the region from the redefinition of American security interests, which China, Japan, and possibly even India will jockey to fill. The other is that the United States may be left in a position of preponderant influence that will work against regional economic and political interests. The tension between these two lines of thinking has so far resulted in an inability on the part of the ASEAN states to define a coherent response beyond a common recognition that the United States should retain a security presence in the region.[93]

U.S. thinking about its security presence in Southeast Asia is more positive than Southeast Asian anxieties would suggest. With the end of the U.S. base relationship with the Philippines, the other ASEAN states and the United States have been working out plans for a continuing presence that will be very different from the relatively large war-fighting capability once centered at Clark air base and Subic naval base near Manila; it should be more acceptable and sustainable, as well. The new arrangements provide for elements of the U.S. Seventh Fleet to be passing through; for its vessels to be making port visits and using shipyards in several countries for repairs; for units of the U.S. air force to be mounting surveillance flights from various locations; for air bases to be kept available for use by big transport planes in the event of a crisis; and for joint exercises to be undertaken by U.S. and ASEAN forces on a bilateral basis. These arrangements involve Indonesia, Malaysia, Singapore, and Thailand in varying degrees—and prospectively the Philippines, as well—with coordination managed from a regional command in Singapore. Over time it seems reasonable to expect that this new sort of presence will be more visible and will make itself felt politically. The principal reservation that has been posed is the degree to which the new system is centered on Singapore, which is already much concerned about its own security. It probably is too much to hope that the U.S. presence in Singapore will make it possible for the government there to ease up on its defense spending. Continuing efforts to balance the U.S. role in Singapore with enhanced arrangements elsewhere would therefore seem highly desirable. It also is important to continue past levels of U.S. training of military personnel and U.S. sales of military equipment. These measures are particularly important in the case of Thailand, where the United States conducted forty joint military exercises, large and small, in one recent year. But they are valuable in some degree to each of the ASEAN states.

The United States can contribute to Southeast Asian security by other forms of presence, as well, of course. Nothing can match the presence of the president of the United States, and Bill Clinton established his presence in the Asia-Pacific region in dramatic fashion in his first year in office. He talked during the presidential campaign of 1992 about the need to build "a new Pacific community." Acting on that vision proved difficult, as crises elsewhere in the world could not be ignored. Nevertheless, his first foreign trip, in July 1993, was to Japan and Korea, and he reaffirmed the U.S. security commitment to both. In November he hosted a get-acquainted meeting of the heads of government of the APEC members in Seattle, at which only Malaysia was not represented, apparently out of pique over the fate of Dr. Mahathir's alternate vision of an East Asia region that excluded Western members. But presidential events will necessarily be few and far between. Visits by U.S. officials, including cabinet members, subcabinet officials, and members of the Senate and House, are all important to perceptions of Washington interest. American business has all along accounted for the bulk of the Americans present in all the ASEAN states except the Philippines. As the Clinton administration takes steps to increase U.S. exports, this American presence should increase in Southeast Asia.

The hard question is whether this will be enough to maintain something like the current balance in the region. One form of additional action that has been proposed on several occasions is a more active military role for Japan in Southeast Asia. A prime minister of Thailand, the only country in the region not occupied by the Japanese in World War II, proposed a few years ago that the Thai and Japanese navies might hold joint exercises. Nothing ever came of that. A vice-minister of Japan in early 1992 floated the idea of a Southeast Asian peacekeeping force, under UN auspices, that would enable Japanese forces to operate in the region and train jointly with regional forces.[94] The prime minister of Malaysia was quoted at the time as suggesting that "Japan on its own shouldn't get involved in any military arrangements with anyone."[95] This history gave increased significance to the absence of any ASEAN objection to the Japanese contribution of an engineering unit to the UN Transitional Authority in Cambodia later in the same year. Commenting on that first involvement of Japanese forces in the region since 1945, an Indonesian security official observed: "We don't make too much of it. It is so much the better for the Japanese to do this and have no one object. Of course, feelings about the Japanese are less strong in Indonesia than in Singapore, Malaysia, and the Philippines."[96] Thus an expanded Japanese military role has so far received only limited support in Southeast Asia. In the present environment, and barring a miscalculation by the Chinese, it does not appear that regional balance is going to be sought in a larger Japanese military role.

The principal form that proposals have taken has been for multilateral consultations on regional security issues. The government of Australia has been calling since 1991 for some sort of regional dialogue on security issues on a Pacific-wide basis. Tokyo also has held the view for several years that some sort of framework is needed to regularize security talks among the governments of the Asia-Pacific region. The leaders of the ASEAN governments, meeting in Singapore in early 1992, decided to add their voices to those of Australia and Japan. They voted to use the annual conference of their foreign ministers with their dialogue partners—the United States, Japan, Canada, Australia, New Zealand, South Korea, and the European Community—as a forum for discussion on regional security.

Washington was initially not comfortable with these proposals. Secretary of State Baker expressed considerable wariness about giving up the "tried and tested" framework of bilateral security relations between the United States and its security partners in the region, as well as apprehension about suggestions that Chinese and Russian representatives be included as equals in the process. A growing consensus, however—one that included many nonofficial Americans—favored U.S. participation in some sort of security discussions in the Asia-Pacific region. The day seemed to have passed when regional anxieties could be laid to rest by assurances from Washington alone, and issues such as territorial disputes and arms limitation were in need of attention.[97]

Many questions remain to be explored in concept or tested in practice. A major issue is what can reasonably be expected in a region that is so full of differences and disparities and that has so little history of regional security discussion. Some fear specifically that there is such distrust between China and Japan that any effort to draw them together will only be polarizing. Meanwhile, others argue that talks might not have to have a lot of operational significance in order to be useful psychologically. According to this view, it might be useful to discuss issues like the South China Sea and arms control even if the issues are not settled. It would be useful to help Japan become better integrated into the region's security as a regular member of the East Asian community. China also faces a serious problem of how, as its power grows, it is going to approach the region and be accepted by it. Talks would be useful if only to begin to build a better understanding among China, Japan, and the United States that they all have a long-term interest in some kind of peaceful accommodation with each other and with the other states of the region. For the United States, the issue also is whether it wants to be counted as "present," to use the words of a Bush administration official, in the hope that "it might make people feel that they need not do some things they would otherwise feel they need to do."[98]

The Clinton administration wisely decided that the ASEAN-sponsored initiative was a place to start. And it was not as though the ASEAN states had had no experience in such matters. The ASEAN ministers and their dialogue partners had talked for years at their annual meetings about Cambodia. The ASEAN initiative on Cambodia was not enough in itself to bring about a political solution there; in the end, that has taken an international conference, the UN Security Council, and a large UN-sponsored presence on the ground—and all of that might not prove to be enough. At the same time, the ASEAN talks did lay essential groundwork, and the ASEAN governments have participated actively in the UN-sponsored activities since. If some kind of peaceful settlement results in Cambodia, the ASEAN governments will deserve much of the credit. Now the ASEAN ministers are concerned about the South China Sea. Regional security talks represent a reasonable undertaking by friends and allies of the United States. By leaving behind the strictures of the past, and agreeing to participate, Washington is contributing to a renewed sense of its serious interest in Southeast Asia.

In May 1993 U.S. officials sat down in Brunei with senior officials of all six ASEAN states for the first time during the Clinton administration. Winston Lord, the U.S. assistant secretary of state for East Asian and Pacific affairs, said he welcomed ASEAN's readiness to address regional security matters. He did suggest that political issues like democracy and human rights, and economic issues like trade and jobs, could not be dealt with as separate matters. They were, in his words, "components of a broader definition of security."[99] Lord also said that the United States would not change its security posture in the Pacific. "We will continue to base our security in the Pacific on our alliances and other bilateral security relationships," Lord said. The United States "will maintain [its] forward deployed forces in the region both to deal with specific contingencies and to contribute to regional stability."[100]

Two months later the members of ASEAN met with their seven dialogue partners at the ministerial level to discuss what was by now known as the ASEAN Regional Forum. China, Russia, Vietnam, and Laos attended as observers. Statements made at the meeting indicated that the main achievement was to begin talking. Secretary of State Christopher affirmed U.S. support for the initiative. The agenda of future meetings is vague, but is expected to develop over time. A possible northeast Asian security forum could affect the geographic scope of the ASEAN-initiated meetings. And experience with efforts to discuss disputes such as those centered in the South China Sea will be important to what functions the meetings acquire. That the venture is experimental is a given.

The United States has nevertheless turned a significant corner in its security relations with Southeast Asia. The U.S. effort at denial that followed the war in Vietnam has ended. Southeast Asians are taking increased responsibility for the security of their region. A new strategic balance is being established in the Asia-Pacific region, and the United States is beginning to demonstrate that it is prepared to play an active role in that process. These are significant achievements for all concerned.

Chapter 8

Weighing the Trade-offs

As this is written, the United States is engaged in a search for its proper role in the world in the wake of the collapse of the Soviet Union. Shorn of the burdens of the Cold War, the American people and their representatives in Washington are considering afresh their priorities as a nation. It is a task made difficult by the enormity of the change that has been wrought in world affairs and by the seeming absence of political leaders able to articulate the issues and opportunities in a manner that captures the historic nature of this moment. In other capitals as well as Washington, political men and women are not finding it easy to define their core values in the new circumstances in which all find themselves. There is a danger in these circumstances that the United States will delay taking any action at all, or out of frustration with the complexity of the problems it faces, take precipitate action that responds to a single dimension of a problem. The world needs a United States that is capable of deliberate and balanced action across a broad front.

A continuing effort will be needed in the United States to bring the federal budget deficit under control. The necessity of doing so seems to be agreed upon, but the extent to which this will be accomplished by spending cuts or tax increases seems likely to be a topic of debate for at least the remainder of the 1990s. A similar

93

effort will be needed to bring the nation's foreign trade into closer balance. As we have shown, righting our trade balance means very largely increasing our exports to East and Southeast Asia. Reducing the budget deficit and increasing our exports are both needed if the United States is to become a creditor nation again, rather than remain the debtor nation it has become. This is of enormous consequence for the rest of the world, and for the U.S. place in it.

Meanwhile, under pressure to reduce its spending, and with no mortal enemy in sight, the United States has been actively reducing its armed forces. While reductions will occur primarily in Europe, it is hard to believe that the Pacific command will be untouched, U.S. official assurances to the contrary notwithstanding. Indeed, from the perspective of Southeast Asia, the U.S. armed forces withdrawal began with the departure of American troops from Vietnam in 1973. The withdrawal has been made virtually complete with the departure of U.S. forces from the Philippines, driven by the volcano that covered the runways of Clark air base and by the equally volcanic vote of the Philippine Senate denying the United States further use of Subic Bay naval base. After almost a century, the United States has no permanent military presence left in Southeast Asia that is any larger than the 200-person logistical command recently established in Singapore.

Encouraged by the return of popular government to much of eastern Europe and the former Soviet Union, Americans also are expressing a new and aggressive interest in the state of democratic governance elsewhere in the world, and this policy is running into particular trouble in Southeast Asia. Until the collapse of communism in eastern Europe, the United States did not in its official policy seem to focus much attention on whether a foreign leader was a dictator or not. A classic case was that of Ferdinand Marcos of the Philippines, who was lauded in a toast by Vice President George Bush in 1981 for his "adherence to democratic principles."[101] With the end of the Cold War, Americans have been able to adopt new criteria in demanding free and fair elections, supporting the rights of opposition parties, and championing freedom of information in other countries. Yet some of the most vociferous opponents of the United States in recent UN conferences on human rights have been several governments of Southeast Asia, among its best friends in the Cold War years.

These developments—the relative decline in the U.S. economic role in the region since the mid-1980s, the visible withdrawal of U.S. air and naval forces from the region, and the rise of opposition to the United States on political questions—represent a dramatic reversal of America's power and influence in Southeast Asia. Any of these developments would not necessarily be damaging in itself. The military withdrawal began from a position in which American forces were overextended, in terms of their political support at home in the case of Vietnam, and in terms of their economic cost in the case of the Philippines. The relative economic decline results in part from the economic rise of others, which could be seen as a positive result of American policies. The political disagreement is only beginning to heat up, and there is still time to seek common ground. But taken together, the changes in the U.S. military, economic, and political position in Southeast Asia signal a need to revise Americans' thinking—about themselves and about Southeast Asia.

What the new situation in Southeast Asia means for Americans is that while the United States is now so powerful that no other nation on earth can cause it grievous harm, it is less influential today than it was only a few years ago. Americans may urge their views on the nations of Southeast Asia, but can have less assurance those views will be accepted. Americans may make proposals, but can have less confidence they will be adopted. The principal reasons for this condition have to do with the American people, with their failure to save and invest, and with their uncertainties about how their armed might is to be used. What the new situation means for Southeast Asians is that they are more autonomous than they have been, thrown more on their own resources, freer to agree or disagree with the United States. These observations are not meant to suggest that there has been a radical alteration in the relationship. The Southeast Asian states want to keep the United States involved in the region as a counterbalance to the presence of others. The balance of power in the region has shifted, however, and so has the weight of American influence. The result is that the United States must do more persuading than in the past, more sharing in consensus-building. This is not a prospect that the lone superpower will accept easily.

Improving American economic relations is a case in point. Improving these relations with East and Southeast Asia is now a high-priority goal of U.S. foreign policy, as enunciated by Secretary of State Christopher in testimony before the Senate Foreign Relations Committee in November 1993. The aim is to establish a "new Pacific community" of trade and integrated economies "in the most lucrative terrain for American exports and jobs."[102] A significant means to that end is the proposed strengthening of the APEC forum, whose leaders gathered in Seattle in the same month on the invitation of President Clinton. The meeting was welcomed by leaders from throughout the Pacific as a sign that the U.S. government did indeed intend to redirect its attention to improving its economic relations with them. At the same time, there was some unease, especially in Japan and Southeast Asia, about American aims beyond that broad goal. A U.S.-led panel of experts fell just short of recommending that the APEC members agree on an ultimate goal of a free trade area.[103] White House officials, briefing reporters prior to the Seattle meeting, threatened to move quickly to develop a trade association with Asia if the Europeans did not make possible a conclusion of the Uruguay Round of GATT negotiations.[104] The APEC group of states is not going to take any such precipitate action, and U.S. trade officials understand this very well. What others in the United States need to understand and accept is that a process is involved—not just the setting of goals, but the evolution of an economic community step by step. The United States will have to learn to participate in that process with patience, and avoid positioning itself out in front of its partners as a matter of course. Progress will come only incrementally if America's Japanese and Southeast Asian partners are to be part of the process too.

Meanwhile, the United States must take steps in its bilateral relations with individual Southeast Asian governments to reduce its trade deficit with their economies, as with the rest of East Asia. The U.S. government will have to involve itself actively and directly in the effort. The strengthening of the Export-Import Bank must be continued. The staff and facilities of the U.S. and Foreign Commercial Service must be enhanced, especially to serve small and medium-size businesses. U.S. government officials must be involved in promoting export sales to public entities in the ASEAN states. All these activities are already incorporated in the Clinton administration's "national export strategy." What is needed is steady implementation of the strategy.

An export promotion campaign will involve some trade-offs for the United States, as well as for the governments of the ASEAN countries. Such a campaign will place the United States in a somewhat different position vis-à-vis individual ASEAN governments than was created by the past emphasis on intellectual property rights and threats of sanctions. The United States will be seeking advantageous decisions from the ASEAN governments, and will want to put the best possible face on the total relationship in order to strengthen its case. As a practical matter, this will involve some give-and-take on both sides.

The ASEAN governments also will face some trade-offs in their relations with the United States in the new economic circumstances. If they are seriously concerned about the rise of Chinese and Japanese influence, they will have an opportunity to contribute to balance among the external powers by keeping U.S. economic interest growing. Similarly, if they are seriously concerned about keeping U.S. air and naval forces active in the region, they will have an opportunity to give the United States a greater economic interest in doing so. Given the current distribution of U.S. trade deficits among the ASEAN economies, the pressure in the short term will be on Thailand and Malaysia. But the problem is general, and all five major ASEAN countries will have to consider what role they can play in helping to right the U.S. trade imbalance.

Secretary of State Christopher took the position in Vienna that human rights, economic interest, and military security are all important. Another way of formulating the position would be to say that better communications with ASEAN on issues of governance and human rights would contribute to better U.S. economic and security relations. The United States and Southeast Asian governments must overcome large obstacles to achieve better communications on these issues, however. The ASEAN governments, while authoritarian in varying degrees, are popular at home. Even neighboring Vietnam, for all its remaining shortcomings, has begun through economic reforms to ease the conditions of life, especially in the south, where the communist takeover in 1975 led to much hardship and flooded the rest of Southeast Asia with political and economic refugees. And Cambodia, thanks to the efforts of ASEAN and the United Nations, now has a government of national unity. Only Burma has experienced little or no improvement in political and economic conditions under a repressive military regime, and U.S. political and economic relations with Burma are all but frozen. Thus, while Americans' sense of democracy may be offended by the prevailing one-party systems, Southeast Asian countries face multiethnic and multireligious populaces that make strong state power the best hope for continued social amity and economic development.

What is most likely to arouse the American people and their representatives in Washington to moral outrage is any occasion on which military personnel fire on unarmed civilians who are doing no more than expressing their opposition to the government. Outbreaks of this kind of violence, such as occurred in East Timor in 1991 and in Bangkok in 1992, have been a part of the political history of Southeast Asia, and the possibility of repetitions cannot be ruled out. Whether welcomed by regional governments or not, the United States has on occasion been able to help tip the balance in favor of limiting the violence or speeding the return to civilian control. It seems fair to say that such action by the United States is now a political given.

But dramatic instances of political violence and the flight of refugees across borders constitute only the tip of the political iceberg. Below lies the bulk of civic life, including the quality of justice that is experienced by the ordinary citizen. It is possible that the government of the United States and friendly governments of the region could find new common ground by exchanging views and experiences in this large—and largely unexamined—area. A key area for U.S. policy is workers' rights.

Here, too, the United States will be more influential in political matters with states with which it enjoys good relations in other fields. Its ability to influence the armed forces of a country in the interest of limiting violence will be greater where it already has good lines of communication with the armed forces. Likewise, when issues of human rights arise, it will have greater influence where U.S. officials have good lines of communication with the political leadership as a result of a wide array of other mutual interests, including aid, trade, and investment. In short, almost everything the United States can do of a positive nature is likely to strengthen its ability to advance its interests in human rights. That is also a way of saying that while the United States must communicate its human rights views strongly, it should be cautious about the use of sanctions. As the case of Burma has shown, sanctions work only when all the key governments concerned impose them, and that unity is extremely difficult to achieve

Southeast Asian governments also must consider economic and security costs and benefits as they approach rights policies. Governments of the region will have a better prospect of keeping the U.S. armed forces active there as a credible counterbalance to other powers if they are working to bridge differences with the United States over political issues. They also will have a better prospect of attracting U.S. government financing for major projects if they are taking some pains to avoid putting themselves into opposition to the United States in highly visible multilateral settings, like the UN human rights conferences in Bangkok and Vienna. They will have to count the potential costs in economic benefits and security relationships of separating themselves from the United States in an area that clearly matters to Americans.

It is possible to enlarge the political common ground between the United States and the countries it counts as friends in Southeast Asia. Doing so will take patience on both sides and a readiness to engage in dialogue. It might even be desirable to begin with governments only in the wings, not at center stage. A deep division of opinion separates many Americans and Southeast Asians, and the sooner steps are taken to try to get them talking with each other, the better. To put the matter in a positive light, every government in Southeast Asia with the exception of Burma's is on record, publicly and privately, as favoring a continuing American economic and security presence in the region. A sense of forward movement in the area of human rights would go a long way toward encouraging support in the United States for a continuing American economic and security presence. This is especially needful in an era in which a relatively weak U.S. executive branch is often on the defensive in attempting to deal with an oppositionist-minded Congress. In addition, the process of dialogue and consensus, which has worked so well in ASEAN affairs, would seem to be well suited to the human rights domain, and would be eminently preferable to the present disposition of the U.S. and ASEAN governments to seek refuge in mutual condemnation. That disposition is better suited to accommodating domestic interest groups than to resolving problems in the international relationship.

We have seen that the end of the Cold War and the departure of American forces from the Philippines has had a dramatic impact on the strategic situation in Southeast Asia. Americans have fought twice in the past half century to protect the interest of the United States in a Southeast Asia that is dominated by no other power or combination of powers. Now it is no longer in a position to protect that interest unaided. In July 1993 Secretary of State Christopher participated in the founding meeting of a regional security forum sponsored by ASEAN and including among its members China, Japan, and Russia. The forum falls far short of being a security organization. It does not provide for its members to exercise the joint use of force, and it is deliberately ambiguous about the longer-term shape the forum might take. But the meeting called attention to the most significant element of the new situation, and that is the extent to which the international order in Southeast Asia depends on the region's own strong, stable, and self-confident nations. This has implications for the United States, as it does for other external powers. Principally it means that the United States, like the rest, will need to give its closest attention in the coming years to the countries that constitute the core of ASEAN, the countries we have identified as the ASEAN four—Indonesia, Thailand, Malaysia, and Singapore. These are the wealthiest countries of the region by most measures, and their economies are its most rapidly growing. They are major purchasers of American goods and services, and their economies should prove even more valuable as the U.S. government increases its focus on export promotion, as it must. These four countries have governments that disagree with the United States on issues of democratic governance, but they are not among the world's serious violators of human rights. On the contrary, they share many values with the American people and are a major source of the foreign students in U.S. colleges and universities. They also are nations that are making available to the United States a variety of air and naval facilities for transit, repairs, and training exercises. For all these reasons, Washington should accord a new level of interest and attention to the ASEAN four.

Indonesia is the country that will test American policy in Southeast Asia the most seriously. Human rights have become a large problem in the relationship. Indonesia's forceful suppression of resistance to its rule in East Timor has been a major issue for some in the United States; dissatisfaction in the U.S. Senate has led to the cancellation of funds for training Indonesian military personnel in the United States and to the banning of the sale of F-5 jet fighters. On the Indonesian side, there is a desire to accommodate the United States, but the flexibility of the government is limited. The Indonesian elite see East Timor as a case of rebellion rather than of rights; even the Indonesian human rights community is not actively concerned. The Indonesians also have alternative sources of military equipment; they have placed an order for jet trainers, estimated at $600 million, with the United Kingdom.

Bilateral relations could continue on their present course. Additional military sales could be banned, but the ban will have limited effect if other nations provide the same materiel. In the absence of joint training or common equipment, joint exercises would cease. The U.S. security commitment to the region would be seriously eroded, and in spite of the high costs, the benefits to East Timor might be minimal. If this scenario is to be avoided, the two governments need to make a major effort to resolve their differences over East Timor. Jakarta already plans to reduce the number of its armed forces personnel in East Timor; it could reduce the sentences of Timorese political prisoners, make East Timor more accessible to foreign visitors, and in other ways begin to normalize the situation. Washington could restore military training and hold out the prospect of access to high-performance aircraft and aerospace technology.

Discussions regarding East Timor also could be pursued in a wider context. Many elements in the bilateral relationship could be enhanced. Indonesia is interested in more U.S. investment in its manufacturing sector; the United States is interested in more U.S. export sales. Jakarta is interested in U.S. attention to the poorest nations in the nonaligned movement; Washington is pressing for fewer restrictions on workers' rights in Indonesia. A presidential review of the relationship also would be timely, given the plans of the APEC members to hold another summit in Indonesia in late 1994. That will be an occasion for the first visit to Indonesia by an American president in almost two decades. For President Soeharto and President Clinton it would be highly desirable on that occasion to have the East Timor issue behind them and relations improving across a broad front.

It is possible to address the other bilateral relationships more briefly. Thailand represents a prime example of a country that should be highly responsive to the Clinton administration's interest in U.S. export expansion. The United States is a major supporter of Thailand's economy, security, and elected civilian government. Americans should be making a major effort to increase U.S. sales to public and private entities in Thailand, and Bangkok should be highly responsive.

Singapore also looks to the United States as its principal foreign investor, principal market, and now principal security partner. The United States has every reason to look to Singapore for some increase in its political openness.

Malaysia was isolated from the rest of the Pacific region in boycotting the informal Seattle summit; that should spell the end of the Malaysian prime minister's ability to sustain interest in an East Asian economic bloc. The United States should now focus on bilateral matters that hold some promise, including full resumption of training in the United States for Malaysia's armed forces, and U.S. sales to balance Malaysia's relatively large trade balance with the United States.

The Philippines needs principally to maintain its emphasis on domestic affairs. It must continue economic policy reform if it is to attract foreign investment and be more competitive in foreign markets. In time it has to decide what political and security relationship it wishes to have with the United States. Washington should respect national feeling in the Philippines by giving the former colony all the time it needs for these processes to run their course.

Vietnam's success with economic reform has been impressive, but the need for foreign aid and trade is substantial. Washington can advance its new priorities in the region by opening diplomatic relations with Vietnam, beginning direct talks on human rights, and granting most favored nation status. None of these steps will be accomplished easily, and so it is desirable that Washington speed the process.

Cambodia needs and deserves substantial and sustained external assistance. As one of the external parties to the peace settlement, the United States must help stabilize the economy, restore basic public services, and build institutions that can provide stability to political and social life.

Burma will receive little or no positive American attention until it takes serious steps toward political and economic reform. The United States should continue to urge other nations to adopt a similar stance.

Thanks to the Seattle summit, the United States is now well along in recognizing the importance of Asia and the Pacific to the revitalization of the U.S. economy and to its own heightened concern for the protection of human rights. The United States is proceeding in an environment in which it also must consider how to contribute to the evolution of a new strategic balance in the region. This is a historic turn for the region and for American policy, and the new goals involve the United States in a highly complex task. The region not only is one of great complexity and divergent interests; it includes many nations whose rapid economic growth has enhanced the self-confidence of their ruling elites, and increased their resistance to American models. The United States is entering on this new period with increased ambitions and reduced economic and political resources.

American policy circles show a tendency to focus attention principally on Japan and China, and in the present atmosphere of nuclear concern, on Korea. U.S. policymakers also must take Southeast Asia seriously into account as it charts its course in Asia-Pacific affairs. The ASEAN economies, although separately managed, are seeking enhanced integration among themselves, and they constitute a growing economic partner of the United States; the ASEAN economies are already a major market for U.S. exports among world regions, and they have the potential to absorb significant increases. ASEAN leaders also have long seen their security as best assured in some degree of alliance or alignment with the United States; they have a distinct and positive role to play in the new strategic balance that lies ahead for the wider region. Southeast Asia also is distinct in that it is still in an early stage of building modern political institutions after a long period of subjection to Western colonial rule; American ideas of human rights have so far found only limited support among national elites. It is hardly necessary to add that the United States has had an unhappy history of intervention in Southeast Asia, and needs to proceed more intelligently if it is to be more successful this next time around.

The United States will have additional reason to take Southeast Asia seriously if, as now seems assured, the nations of Asia and the Pacific are to be engaged in the coming years in a major effort at regional organization, and the United States is to be centrally engaged in that effort. The informal Seattle meeting of political leaders in November 1993 greatly strengthened the U.S. commitment to regionalism in the Pacific. The APEC forum is still in the early stages of formulating its goals, and the Southeast Asian members have made it clear that they will play a significant role in determining the speed with which that process moves ahead. They also have played a creative role in sponsoring the ASEAN Regional Forum for political and security talks, the first multilateral security discussions including all the major states of the Pacific.

There is, then, a new Southeast Asia, as well as a new American agenda, and the United States will do well to give serious attention to the former as it aims to advance the latter.

NOTES

1. David Joel Steinberg, ed., *In Search of Southeast Asia: A Modern History* (New York: Praeger Publishers, 1971).
2. Ibid., p. 274.
3. For an introduction to Philippine society and history, see David Joel Steinberg, *The Philippines: A Singular and a Plural Place* (Boulder, Colo.: Westview, 1990). For an account of Philippine-American relations over time, see James C. Thomson, Jr., Peter W. Stanley, and John Curtis Perry, *Sentimental Imperialists: The American Experience in East Asia* (New York: Harper & Row, 1981). For a review of more recent history of the Philippines and

Philippine-American relations, see John Bresnan, ed., *Crisis in the Philippines: The Marcos Era and Beyond* (Princeton, N.J.: Princeton University Press, 1986).

4. On this period and later, see Evelyn Colbert, *Southeast Asia in International Politics, 1941–1956* (Ithaca, N.Y.: Cornell University Press, 1977).
5. Ibid.
6. For an introduction to the outcome of the war and issues remaining for the United States, see Frederick Z. Brown, *Second Chance: The United States and Indochina in the 1990s* (New York: Council on Foreign Relations, 1989).
7. U.S. National Committee for Pacific Economic Cooperation, *Pacific Economic Outlook 1993–1994*, relevant country chapters (San Francisco, 1993).
8. Adam Gelb et al., *Oil Windfalls: Blessing or Curse?* (New York: Oxford University Press, for the World Bank, 1988).
9. World Bank, *World Development Report 1992* (New York: Oxford University Press, 1992), Table 9.
10. Ibid., Table 23.
11. Investments are not reported by governments in ways that make systematic comparison possible. The government of Indonesia does not include the oil and gas industry in its data on foreign investment at all, considering foreign companies in this industry contractors rather than investors. The government of Malaysia considers investment by a U.S. subsidiary in Singapore to be an investment from Singapore, not one from the United States. The U.S. Department of Commerce reports U.S. investment abroad on a historical-cost basis, which means that it substantially underrepresents the value of investments made in past decades. The government of Japan has changed its definition of foreign investment several times in recent decades, adding a further obstacle to systematic comparison. These and other differences regarding what constitutes investment and how it is counted make cross-national comparisons in the region quite impossible. For a technical discussion, see U.S. International Trade Commission, *East Asia: Regional Economic Integration and Implications for the United States*, 1993, pp. B-3 to B-5; and United Nations Centre for Transnational Corporations, *World Investment Directory 1992*, vol. 1, pp. 39–44.
12. Embassy of the United States of America, *U.S. Investment Survey: Indonesia, September 1991* (Jakarta, 1991).
13. *Far Eastern Economic Review*, December 24–31, 1992.
14. Embassy of the United States of America, *U.S. Investment in Malaysia, June, 1992* (Kuala Lumpur, 1992).
15. Company reports to stockholders.
16. U.S. Department of Commerce, *Survey of Current Business*, vol. 72, no. 8 (August 1992).
17. Embassy of the United States of America, *U.S. Investment in Malaysia.*
18. Linda Y. C. Lim and Pang Eng Fong, *Foreign Direct Investment and Industrialization in Malaysia, Singapore, Taiwan and Thailand* (Paris: Organization for Economic Cooperation and Development, 1991).
19. Office of Trade and Investment Analysis, International Trade Administration, U.S. Department of Commerce, *U.S. Foreign Trade Highlights 1991* (Washington, D.C., 1993).

20. See, for example, Lester Thurow, *Head to Head: The Coming Economic Battle among Japan, Europe, and America* (New York: William Morrow and Company, 1992), and Jeffrey E. Garten, *A Cold Peace: America, Japan, Germany, and the Struggle for Supremacy* (New York: Times Books, 1992).
21. Stephen Guisinger, "Foreign Direct Investment Flows in East and Southeast Asia: Policy Issues," *ASEAN Economic Bulletin*, vol. 8, no. 1 (July 1991), Table 1.
22. Bank of Thailand Monthly Economic Report, February 1992, Table 45, p. 74, cited in United States and Foreign Commercial Service, *Thailand: Country Marketing Plan FY1993* (Bangkok, 1992), p. 3.
23. Guisinger, "Foreign Direct Investment Flows," Table 1.
24. U.S. International Trade Commission, *East Asia: Regional Economic Integration and Implications for the United States* (Washington, D.C., 1993), Figures 5.4 and 5.5.
25. United States and Foreign Commercial Service, *Thailand*, p. 3.
26. Shojiro Tokunaga in Shojiro Tokunaga, ed., *Japan's Foreign Investment and Asian Economic Interdependence: Production, Trade, and Financial Systems* (Tokyo: University of Tokyo Press, 1992), p. 9.
27. Ibid., pp. 9–10.
28. Guisinger, "Foreign Direct Investment Flows," p. 33.
29. Tokonuga, *Japan's Foreign Investment*, p. 17.
30. Ibid., p. 19.
31. For a discussion of this and other issues surrounding Japanese aid, see Dennis T. Yasutomo, *The Manner of Giving: Strategic Aid and Japanese Foreign Policy* (Lexington, Mass.: D.C. Heath, 1986); Shafiqul Islam, ed., *Yen for Development: Japanese Foreign Aid and the Politics of Burden-Sharing* (New York: Council on Foreign Relations Press, 1991); and Margee J. Ensign, *Doing Good or Doing Well? Japan's Foreign Aid Program* (New York: Columbia University Press, 1992).
32. Tokonuga, *Japan's Foreign Investment*, p. 24.
33. Ibid., p. 19.
34. Ibid., pp. 20–24.
35. Lim and Fong, *Foreign Direct Investment*.
36. Kiichi Miyazawa, "The New Era of the Asia-Pacific and Japan-ASEAN Cooperation," Bangkok, January 16, 1993 (provisional translation released by the Foreign Ministry, Government of Japan).
37. Personal communication, Bangkok, August 13, 1992.
38. Personal communication, Bangkok, August 15, 1992.
39. Personal communication, Bangkok, August 13, 1992.
40. Personal communication, Bangkok, August 15, 1992.
41. Office of the United States Trade Representative, *1992 National Trade Estimate Report on Foreign Trade Barriers* (Washington, D.C., 1992), pp. 239–244.
42. Personal communication, Washington, D.C., February 17, 1993.
43. Personal communication, Bangkok, August 14, 1992.
44. Personal communication, New York, March 2, 1992.
45. Personal communication, August 1992.
46. Personal communication, Bangkok, August 15, 1993.

47. Personal communication, Washington, D.C., February 17, 1993.
48. *New York Times*, September 28, 1993.
49. Lawrence B. Krause, *U.S. Economic Policy Toward the Association of Southeast Asian Nations: Meeting the Japanese Challenge* (Washington, D.C.: Brookings Institution, 1982).
50. U.S. International Trade Commission, *East Asia*, pp. 142–148.
51. *Far Eastern Economic Review*, July 11, 1991.
52. *Far Eastern Economic Review*, November 28, 1991.
53. *Nihon Keizai*, November 25, 1991.
54. *Far Eastern Economic Review*, November 28, 1991.
55. Khaw Guat Hoon, "The International Politics of Southeast Asia: Issues in 1989," in *Southeast Asian Affairs: 1990* (Singapore: Institute of Southeast Asian Studies, 1990), p. 21.
56. *The Asian Wall Street Journal Weekly*, June 14, 1993.
57. Seiji Naya et al., *ASEAN–U.S. Initiative: Assessment and Recommendations for Improved Economic Relations* (Honolulu and Singapore: East-West Center and Institute for Southeast Asian Studies, 1989).
58. Personal communication, Manila, January 15, 1993.
59. *Far Eastern Economic Review*, December 10, 1992.
60. *Far Eastern Economic Review*, June 17, 1993.
61. Ibid.
62. *New York Times*, June 15, 1993.
63. Ibid.
64. *Far Eastern Economic Review*, May 27, 1993.
65. Personal communication, Bangkok, August 1992.
66. Human Rights Watch, *Human Rights Watch World Report 1993* (New York, 1993), p. 153.
67. Ibid., pp. 153–157.
68. Personal communication, Jakarta, September 1992.
69. *New York Times*, March 14, 1993.
70. *New York Times*, April 11, 1993.
71. Derek Da Cunha, "Major Asian Powers and the Development of the Singaporean amd Malaysian Armed Forces," in D. da Cunha and N. A. Kamal, eds., *Strategic Development in the Asia-Pacific*, a special issue of *Contemporary Southeast Asia*, vol. 13, no. 1 (June 1991), pp. 57–71.
72. Personal communication, Singapore, September 1992.
73. Research Institute for Peace and Security, *Asian Security*, annual volumes; Richard Stubbs, "Malaysian Defence Policy: Strategy versus Structure," in da Cunha and Kamal, *Strategic Development; Far Eastern Economic Review*, April 30, 1992, and May 13, 1993; and *Asian Wall Street Journal Weekly*, July 5, 1993.
74. Personal communication, Kuala Lumpur, August 1992; and *Far Eastern Economic Review*, February 18, 1993.
75. Research Institute for Peace and Security, *Asian Security*, annual volumes; Stubbs, "Malaysian Defence Policy," personal communication, Bangkok, August 1992; and *Far Eastern Economic Review*, April 30, 1992, and March 11, 1993.
76. Personal communication, Jakarta, September 1993.

77. Chin Kin Wah, ed., *Defence Spending in Southeast Asia* (Singapore: Institute of Southeast Asian Studies, 1987), appendix E.
78. *Far Eastern Economic Review*, May 13, 1993.
79. Personal communication, Manila, January 1993.
80. Personal communication, Manila, September 1993.
81. *New York Times*, July 27, 1993.
82. See, for example, Stephen Bosworth, "The United States in Asia," *Foreign Affairs*, vol. 71, no. 1, 1991/92, pp. 113–129.
83. See, for example, Richard Betts, "Wealth, Power, and Instability: East Asia after the Cold War," *International Security*, vol. 18, no. 3 (Winter 1993–94) pp. 34–77.
84. Hadi Soesastro, *Implications of the Post–Cold War Politico-Security Environment for the Pacific Economy* (New York: East Asian Institute, Columbia University, 1993).
85. Personal communication, New York, April 13, 1992.
86. Robert A. Scalapino, "The U.S. and Asia: Future Prospects," *Foreign Affairs*, vol. 70, no. 5 (Winter 1991/92), pp. 19–40; and Paul Kreisberg, "The U.S. and Asia in 1990," *Asian Survey*, vol. 31, no. 1 (January 1991), pp. 1–13.
87. *Far Eastern Economic Review*, May 27, 1993.
88. Muthiah Alagappa, "The Major Powers and Southeast Asia," *International Journal*, vol. 44, no. 3 (Summer 1989), pp. 541–597.
89. Lee Poh Ping, "Japan and the Asia-Pacific Region" (paper for the Woodrow Wilson Center Conference on Japan and the World, January 27–28, 1992).
90. See, for example, Lee Kuan Yew, Singapore Senior Minister, Keynote Speech, Kansai Zaikai seminar, Kyoto, Japan. Cited in *Straits Times*, February 14, 1992.
91. Personal communication, September 1992.
92. Personal communication, September 1992.
93. Chin Kin Wah, "ASEAN and the Major Powers" (paper for the Asia Pacific Forum Conference on ASEAN Internal and External Cooperation in the 1990s and Beyond, Manila, January 13–15, 1993).
94. *Far Eastern Economic Review*, January 30, 1992.
95. *Asian Wall Street Journal*, February 3, 1992.
96. Personal communication, Jakarta, September 1993.
97. Bosworth, "The United States in Asia."
98. Personal communication, New York, May 1992.
99. Reuters, May 15, 1993.
100. Knight-Ridder, May 17, 1993.
101. Stanley Karnow, *In Our Image: America's Empire in the Philippines* (New York: Random House, 1989), p. 401.
102. *Washington Post*, November 5, 1993.
103. In the face of much opposition, the panel limited itself to recommending "an ultimate goal of free trade within the region." See C. Fred Bergsten et al., *A Vision for APEC: Towards an Asia Pacific Economic Community*. Report of the Eminent Persons Group to APEC Ministers, October 1993, p. 63.
104. *New York Times*, November 16, 1993.

Index